QUESTIONS & ANSWERS:
PROFESSIONAL RESPONSIBILITY

QUESTIONS & ANSWERS:
Professional Responsibility

Multiple-Choice and Short-Answer
Questions and Answers

Third Edition

PATRICK EMERY LONGAN
William Augustus Bootle Chair in Ethics and
Professionalism in the Practice of Law
Walter F. George School of Law
Mercer University

ISBN: 978-1-4224-9860-6

NOTE TO USERS
To ensure that you are using the latest materials available in this area, please be sure to periodically check the LexisNexis Law School web site for downloadable updates and supplements at www.lexisnexis.com/lawschool.

Editorial Offices
121 Chanlon Rd., New Providence, NJ 07974 (908) 464-6800
201 Mission St., San Francisco, CA 94105-1831 (415) 908-3200
www.lexisnexis.com

MATTHEW◆BENDER

(2012–Pub.3179)

ABOUT THE AUTHOR

Patrick Emery Longan holds the William Augustus Bootle Chair in Ethics and Professionalism in the Practice of Law at Mercer University's Walter F. George School of Law and is the Director of the Mercer Center for Legal Ethics and Professionalism (www.law.mercer.edu/mclep). Professor Longan is a 1983 graduate of the University of Chicago Law School, which he attended after obtaining his undergraduate degree from Washington University in St. Louis and his Master's degree in economics from the University of Sussex. Upon graduation from law school, Professor Longan clerked for Bernard M. Decker, Senior United States District Judge for the Northern District of Illinois, practiced law for seven years, and became a full-time law teacher in 1991. He lives in Macon, Georgia, with his wife, Gretchen, and their family.

PREFACE

The study of Professional Responsibility requires law students to examine the many and often conflicting roles that lawyers play. Lawyers act on behalf of clients, but they also have duties to the courts, to third parties, to their law partners and associates, and to their own consciences. This subject requires students to ask fundamental questions about the profession they have chosen to enter. What duties does a lawyer owe a client? How far can a lawyer go to help a client? What can or should the lawyer be able to tell others about the client's past or planned misdeeds? What strategies or tactics are permissible in helping a client? When does the lawyer's duty to the system of justice become paramount? How does a lawyer balance conflicts between the interests of a client and the lawyer's own interests? How does a lawyer balance conflicts between a client and another client, or between a client and future clients? These and similar questions require law students to place themselves in the roles they soon will play for real clients and to learn the accepted boundaries of a lawyer's duties and responsibilities.

Professional Responsibility also involves the obligations of judges. Members of the judiciary also have many conflicting duties. They must decide cases fairly but expeditiously, and in the process they must be courteous and civil to counsel and parties. Judges must sit unless they are disqualified, but in certain circumstances they must recuse themselves. They are expected to be involved in extra-judicial activities, but those activities are highly regulated to protect the integrity of the judicial process. Judges must navigate these complex tradeoffs in order to ensure the quality, the fairness, and the appearance of the administration of justice.

The questions and answers in this book are based upon the American Bar Association's Model Rules of Professional Conduct and the ABA's Model Code of Judicial Conduct. Your state's rules for lawyers and judges will differ somewhat from these, but the model provisions have proven to be quite influential in the development of many states' rules. The questions and answers in this book reflect the text and interpretations of the Model Rules and Model Code as of September 30, 2011.

The questions in this book raise these issues in specific factual circumstances. They will best serve your purpose if you will use them as a supplement to the casebook and other materials assigned by your Professional Responsibility professor. This book is not a substitute for those materials, nor is it a "short course" on Professional Responsibility. It is intended to enable you to test your understanding and adapt your study strategies accordingly. For the book to be useful, it is essential that you study the applicable Model Rules of Professional Conduct or the applicable provisions of the Model Code of Judicial Conduct before attempting to answer the questions. You will find the official comments to these provisions essential reading as well. Read the questions carefully and attempt to answer them before you read the suggested answer. You will learn more from that active endeavor than you will from the passive exercise of reading the question and then flipping to the suggested answer.

I wish you well as you undertake the study of your responsibilities as a member of your chosen profession.

Patrick Longan
Macon, Georgia
October 2011

TABLE OF CONTENTS

QUESTIONS

1. A lawyer represents a client in a divorce and child custody case. The client tells the lawyer that her husband is very protective of his elderly parents and that, if the lawyer will subpoena the parents for depositions, the husband is much more likely to be reasonable in negotiations. The lawyer knows that the parents do have relevant, discoverable information regarding custody issues, but the lawyer firmly believes that the depositions would do more harm (to the parents and to the negotiation process) than good. Which of the following statements most accurately describes the lawyer's obligations and/or options under the Model Rules of Professional Conduct?

   (A) The lawyer must consult with the client about the benefits and detriments of taking the depositions but then may seek to withdraw if the lawyer has a fundamental disagreement with the client's instructions.

   (B) The lawyer must consult with the client about the benefits and detriments of taking the depositions but then has the authority to decide whether or not he should take them.

   (C) The lawyer must exercise his independent professional judgment about whether it would be in his client's interests to take the depositions.

   (D) The lawyer must consult with the client about the benefits and detriments of taking the depositions but then must follow the client's instructions regarding whether or not to take them.

2. A lawyer is representing a defendant in an employment discrimination case. The lawyer receives a settlement demand from the plaintiff. The lawyer believes that the settlement demand is excessive and expects her client to reject it. Which of the following most accurately states the lawyer's obligations under the Model Rules of Professional Conduct?

   (A) The lawyer must communicate the demand to her client unless the client has previously indicated that such a demand would be excessive.

   (B) The lawyer must communicate the demand to the client and give the client the benefit of her professional judgment and candid advice about the excessiveness of the demand.

   (C) The lawyer must communicate the demand to the client and give the client the benefit of her professional judgment and candid advice about the excessiveness of the demand, unless the client has previously indicated that such a demand would be excessive.

   (D) The lawyer must communicate the demand to her client.

3. A lawyer who specializes in criminal defense work is approached by a prospective client

who has been indicted for money laundering. The lawyer has handled many such cases and his customary flat fee is $50,000, which is equal to the prevailing market rate in his community for defense of complex crimes. The client, however, only has about $50,000 in liquid assets, and the trial is not expected to be complete for many months. The client cannot find work because of the pendency of the charges. Which of the following statements most accurately describes the lawyer's options under the Model Rules of Professional Conduct?

(A) The lawyer may accept the case on a contingent basis and charge more than the standard $50,000.

(B) The lawyer may charge the standard $50,000 but then loan the money back to the client to allow the client to have money to live on.

(C) The lawyer may decline the case because the client cannot afford his usual fee.

(D) The lawyer must accept the client's case for a reduced fee unless doing so would cause the lawyer to suffer an unreasonable financial burden.

4. A public defender is representing the defendant in a murder case. In investigating the case, the public defender gathers indisputable evidence from a relative of the client that the client committed a murder for which another man has been sentenced to life in prison without parole. Which of the following statements best describes the lawyer's options under the Model Rules of Professional Conduct?

(A) The lawyer must disclose her client's guilt if she reasonably believes that doing so is necessary to remedy the wrongful conviction of the other man.

(B) The lawyer may disclose her client's guilt because the information is not covered by the attorney-client privilege.

(C) The lawyer may not disclose his client's guilt without her client's permission because that is information relating to the representation of her client.

(D) The lawyer may disclose her client's guilt if she reasonably believes that doing so is necessary to prevent substantial bodily harm to the innocent man.

5. The law firm of A & K has office in many cities in the United States. Lawyers in its Dallas office represent Hanafil, Inc. in connection with that company's efforts to purchase the assets of another company. Lawyers in the Seattle office of the firm have been asked to represent a new client in connection with a lawsuit that this client wishes to file against Hanafil, Inc. Which of the following statements most accurately describes the law firm's options under the Model Rules of Professional Conduct?

(A) The firm may undertake the new representation because the matters are unrelated.

(B) The firm may not undertake the new matter.

(C) The firm may not undertake the new matter without the informed consent of Hanafil and the new Seattle client.

(D) The firm may undertake the new representation because the matters are being handled by offices in different cities.

6. A female attorney regularly represents men in divorce cases. The attorney has fallen in love with a client in the midst of a case, and the two of them are discussing whether it would be appropriate to begin a sexual relationship. Which of the following most accurately describes the lawyer's options under the Model Rules of Professional Conduct?

(A) The lawyer may commence a consensual sexual relationship with her client.

(B) The lawyer may not commence a sexual relationship with her client while he is a client.

(C) The lawyer may commence a sexual relationship with her client as long as by doing so she is not unfairly exploiting her fiduciary role and using her client's trust to his disadvantage.

(D) The lawyer may commence a sexual relationship with her client as long as she obtains the client's informed consent, confirmed in writing, to the conflict of interest that is created by the sexual relationship.

7. Alexander Abrams is an associate at a multinational law firm. He has interviewed for a job with the small, boutique firm of Levarge & Monahan (L & M). His possible employment by L & M has hit a snag, however, because L & M has realized that Alexander has done work for clients of his current firm on several cases (the "Common Cases") in which L & M represents the opposing party. L & M wants to hire Alexander but will not risk creating a conflict of interest in its representations of its clients in the Common Cases. Which of the following statements most accurately describes L & M's options under the Model Rules of Professional Conduct?

(A) L & M may hire Alexander if it screens him from any involvement in the Common Cases.

(B) L & M may not hire Alexander because he would create a conflict of interest within L & M.

(C) L & M may hire Alexander.

(D) L & M may hire Alexander only if all parties to the Common Cases consent and that consent is confirmed in writing.

8. George Valiant is a new associate in Peabody and Falmouth (PF), a large urban law firm. He works in the corporate department. PF has just been asked to represent a defendant in a large products liability case. A routine conflicts check alerted PF to the fact that George's wife, Nancy Valiant, is the lead counsel for the opposing party in that case. Which of the following statements most accurately reflects PF's options with respect to undertaking the new representation?

(A) The firm may not undertake the new representation without consent of its client because George has a conflict of interest that will be imputed to all the lawyers in the firm.

(B) The firm may undertake the new representation because George will not be working on the case and therefore the firm does not have a conflict of interest.

(C)   The firm may undertake the case as long as the firm formally screens George from any involvement in the case, notifies the opposing party of the screens, and certifies to its client that George has been screened.

(D)   The firm may undertake the new representation because George's conflict will not be imputed to other lawyers in the firm.

9.   An attorney is outside counsel to Solar Panels, Inc. (SPI), a company that is engaged in the design and production of experimental solar panels for the generation of electricity in the American southwest. A new president of SPI instructs the lawyer to investigate rumors that SPI has defrauded its customers with false reports of the efficiency and cost-effectiveness of SPI's products. The attorney conducts the investigation and concludes that the allegations are true and that SPI perpetrated this fraud without the knowledge or assistance of any of its lawyers. The attorney strongly believes that it is in SPI's interest to reveal publicly what the prior management of the company did, in order to try to protect the company's credibility with investors, the government, and the public. The attorney is further convinced that continued silence would cause enormous harm to the company when the truth inevitably comes out. The attorney takes his concerns to the officers and Board of Directors of SPI, but the attorney is instructed to remain silent. Which of the following statements most accurately reflects the attorney's options under the Model Rules of Professional Conduct?

(A)   The attorney may not reveal the information because the client has refused to consent to the disclosure.

(B)   The attorney may not reveal the fraud publicly because the lawyer's services were not used in connection with the fraud and the attorney learned the information while conducting an investigation for SPI.

(C)   The attorney may reveal the information publicly because the attorney reasonably believes that doing so is necessary to prevent substantial injury to the organization.

(D)   The attorney may reveal the information because the client has perpetrated a fraud that caused substantial financial injury to others.

10.   An attorney represents a class of thousands plaintiffs in a consumer credit case. He has just been diagnosed with cancer. Which of the following statements most accurately describes the attorney's responsibilities under the Model Rules of Professional Conduct?

(A)   The lawyer must immediately cease his activities on behalf of the class and inform the members of the class that he has withdrawn.

(B)   The lawyer may withdraw from the representation if his physical condition materially impairs his ability to represent the class.

(C)   The lawyer must disclose his physical condition to the named representative of the class and may continue to represent the class only with the representative's informed consent, confirmed in writing.

(D) The lawyer must seek to withdraw from the representation if his physical condition materially impairs his ability to represent the class.

11. Butch Bauman is an elderly widower who lives at the Autumn Leaves Nursing Home. Mike Steel has been Butch's attorney for many years. Butch recently had a stroke that has impaired his thinking. Mike knows that for years Butch's step-daughter has been pestering him to sign Butch's house over to her, and on his last visit to Autumn Leaves Mike interrupted a visit by the step-daughter. As Mike walked in, he could see the step-daughter had some kind of papers in her hand and was holding Butch's hand, with a pen in it, up to the papers as if helping him to sign his name. When Mike arrived, the step-daughter abruptly left and refused to speak to Mike or tell him what she was doing. Which of the following statements most accurately reflects Mike's options under the Model Rules of Professional Conduct?

(A) Mike may take reasonably necessary action to protect his client if he obtains consent from the client to reveal the confidential information that makes the action appropriate.

(B) Mike must, as far as reasonably possible, maintain a normal lawyer-client relationship with his client.

(C) Mike must seek to have a guardian appointed for his client.

(D) Mike may take reasonably necessary action to protect his client if his client cannot act adequately in his own interest.

12. Steve Katz is a lawyer and a partner in Katz & Morgan (KM), and he meets with Dana Rogers, a prospective new client. Dana is there to discuss a dispute that she is having with her business partner, Roger Wilson. As is his custom, Steve opens the conversation with an open-ended question, "What brings you here to see me today?" In response, Dana pours forth all the issues that have arisen between her and Roger, including several facts that will be significantly harmful to any attempt by Dana to obtain any legal remedy against Roger. At the end of the meeting, Steve tells Dana about his fee structure, and she tells him that he is too expensive. The next week, Roger comes to Steve and asks Steve to represent him in his dispute with Dana. Which of the following statements most accurately describes the options that Steve and KM have under the Model Rules of Professional Conduct?

(A) Steve and KM may represent Roger against Dana.

(B) Steve may not represent Dana but KM may do so as long as Steve is screened from any participation in the case, receives no income from the case, and Dana is given written notice.

(C) Steve and KM may represent Roger as long as Steve does not use or reveal any of the information he gained from his interview with Dana.

(D) Neither Steve nor KM may represent Roger in this dispute against Dana.

13. Jewel Jackson is a lawyer who routinely requires her clients pay a "retainer" of $2500 at the beginning of any new matter. Jewel places the "retainer" in her firm's trust account. The retainer is really just a deposit, and Jewel bills $250 per hour against the deposit until

it is depleted, and then Jewel routinely asks for an additional deposit. Jewel represented Greg Fox in a matter and followed her usual procedures. Jewel spent 10 hours on the matter, but before she could withdraw the retainer from the trust account, Greg notified Jewel that he thought the $2500 should be returned to him. Which of the following statements most accurately describes Jewel's obligations under the Model Rules of Professional Conduct?

(A) Jewel must keep the funds separate until the dispute is resolved.

(B) Jewel may withdraw the funds because the fees have been earned.

(C) Jewel must remit the funds to the client who claims them.

(D) Jewel must interplead the funds so that a court can resolve the dispute over them.

14. Clayton Ford is a lawyer who has been asked to represent Jimmy Bonner, a college student who has been accused of conspiracy to distribute illegal drugs. Clayton immediately discovers, however, that his law partner has undertaken representation Jimmy's room-mate, who has been charged with being part of the same conspiracy and who has offered to testify against all the other alleged co-conspirators, including Jimmy, in exchange for leniency. Which of the following statements most accurately describes Clayton's options under the Model Rules of Professional Conduct?

(A) Clayton may represent Jimmy because Clayton does not personally represent Jimmy's roommate.

(B) Clayton may not represent Jimmy.

(C) Clayton may represent Jimmy as long as Clayton and his law partner are each screened from any involvement in the other's case.

(D) Clayton may represent Jimmy as long as Jimmy and his roommate each give informed consent to the representation.

15. Edward is a lawyer who routinely defends pharmaceutical companies in product liability actions. Edward is currently representing the co-defendants ABEX, Inc. (AI) and EMU Laboratories Corp. (ELC) in a case involving an alleged defect in a medicine to treat ringworm. AI has now instructed Edward to file a cross-claim against ELC for indemnity. The cross-claim would allege that ELC bears all responsibility for the loss because of a failure to properly test and/or analyze the test results for the medicine. Which of the following statements most accurately describes Edward's options under the Model Rules of Professional Conduct?

(A) Edward may file the cross-claim as long as both clients give informed consent.

(B) Edward may file the cross-claim.

(C) Edward may not file the cross-claim for one client against another client.

(D) Edward may have the cross-claim filed by one of his partners.

16. Elsie Todsen is a lawyer who at one time represented the Bobbitt Air Conditioning Company (BACC) in connection with negotiations arising out of an accident involving John DeGarmo. Before the negotiations were complete, BACC discharged Elsie. John has now asked Elsie to file suit on his behalf against BACC for the same accident. Which of the following statements most accurately describes Elsie's options under the Model Rules of Professional Conduct?

   (A) Elsie may not under any circumstances sue her former client in the same matter in which she formerly represented that client.

   (B) Elsie may not personally represent John but her firm may do so as long as Elsie is screened from any participation in the matter and receives no part of the fee.

   (C) Elsie may not represent John without BACC's informed consent, confirmed in writing.

   (D) Elsie may represent John as long as she reasonably believes that in doing so she can protect BACC's confidential information.

17. Michelle DuPont is an attorney who until recently was a partner in the law firm of Dwight & Richards (D & R). Because of a dispute over her share of D & R's profits, Michelle recently left the firm and started her own firm. Michelle took her biggest client, Tom's Technology Services, Inc. (TTS), with her, including all the matters on which D & R was working for TTS at the time of Michelle's departure. One of those matters was a suit against TTS for installation of a defective set of computer servers at Goliad Enterprises (GE). When Michelle left the firm, she took with her as employees of her new firm all of the lawyers who had confidential information about any of TTS's matters except Joey Oberlin, a young associate who had helped with the GE v. TTS litigation. Now, GE has asked D & R to represent GE in its litigation against TTS. It is clear that TTS will not consent to this. Which of the following statements most accurately states D & R's options under the Model Rules of Professional Conduct?

   (A) D & R may undertake the representation of GE as long as Oberlin is screened from any participation in the case and receives no part of the fee from it.

   (B) D & R may not undertake the new representation because it would be switching sides in the GE v. TTS litigation.

   (C) D & R may not undertake the new representation because Oberlin is still with the firm.

   (D) D & R may undertake the new representation because TTS is no longer a client of the firm.

18. Lawyer Carleton McAllister represents criminal defendants. As a favor to an old friend, Carleton agrees to represent the friend's indigent nephew on murder charges in a notorious case. Carleton agrees to waive his usual fee but needs to expend considerable sums to conduct investigations regarding both the guilt and the sentencing phases. The client does not have the money to pay these expenses. Which of the following best states Carleton's options under the Model Rules of Professional Conduct?

   (A) Carleton may pay the expenses himself.

(B)   Carleton may acquire the literary rights to the nephew's story and pay the expenses from the royalties earned later on the use of those rights.

(C)   Carleton may advance the costs of the expenses himself but must obtain the client's agreement to repay the sums advanced.

(D)   Carleton may not pay or advance the expenses because that is prohibited financial assistance to a client.

19.   Jenna Weatherby was an attorney with the State Department of Transportation (SDOT). As a junior lawyer for SDOT, she helped her superiors to brief various issues that came before the courts related to the controversial expansion of Arbor Road in Capitol City. Her work supported the expansion. Now that she is in private practice, Jenna has been asked by the Chamber of Commerce of Capitol City to represent it as an intervenor in litigation brought against SDOT by Citizen Opposed to Arbor Road Expansion (COARE) to stop the expansion. The Chamber would be intervening to argue in favor of the expansion of Arbor Road. Which of the following most accurately states Jenna's options under the Model Rules of Professional Conduct?

(A)   Jenna may represent the Chamber because her new client is on the same side of this controversy as her former client.

(B)   Jenna may represent the Chamber because she was not lead counsel for SDOT.

(C)   Jenna may not represent the Chamber without the informed consent of SDOT.

(D)   Jenna may not represent the Chamber.

20.   Pamela Harper is an attorney who recently had the misfortune to be a defendant in a legal malpractice case. Because that experience was so terrible, she would like to obtain routinely from her clients advance waivers of claims against her for malpractice. Which of the following statements most accurately describes Pamela's options under the Model Rules of Professional Conduct?

(A)   Pamela may obtain an enforceable advance waiver of claims against her for malpractice if she provides sufficient information to enable the client to give informed consent.

(B)   Pamela may obtain an enforceable advance waiver of claims against her for malpractice only if her client is independently represented in making the agreement.

(C)   Pamela may obtain an enforceable advance waiver of claims against her for malpractice as long as the client is informed in writing of the desirability of seeking, and is given a reasonable opportunity to seek, the advice of independent legal counsel.

(D)   Pamela cannot obtain an enforceable advance waiver of claims against her for malpractice.

21.   Kara Brown is a new attorney at the Law Offices of Nagy & Nagy (NN). The firm specializes in criminal defense but typically does not represent those accused of violence against women. To her surprise, one day Kara comes to work and discovers that the firm has assigned her to work on the defense of Grover Wellington III, a young man who has

been accused in a brutal sexual assault at the local college. Because of personal experiences, Kara is unable to render competent and diligent representation to anyone accused of such a crime. Which of the following statements most accurately describes the firm's options with respect to its representation of Wellington?

(A) The firm may represent Wellington as long as Kara does not participate in the case.

(B) The firm may not represent Wellington because Kara has a conflict of interest that will be imputed to all the lawyers in the firm.

(C) The firm may represent Wellington as long as Kara is screened from participation in the case and receives no part of the fee therefrom.

(D) Kara and the firm may represent Wellington as long as the client gives informed consent to Kara's conflict.

22. Leah Peterson is an attorney who specializes in estate planning. Her long-time client, Jacob Daniels, who is not related to Leah, has come to her and asked her to revise his will, now that Jacob's wife and children have all predeceased him. Jacob tells Leah that he would like to make a substantial bequest to Leah's daughter for purposes of her education. Which of the following most accurately describes Leah's obligations under the Model Rules of Professional Conduct?

(A) Leah may prepare Jacob's revised will to provide the bequest as long as Jacob gives his informed consent to the gift to Leah's daughter and as long as Leah reasonably believes that Jacob has the mental capacity to give that consent.

(B) Leah may not prepare the new will if it contains a substantial bequest to her daughter.

(C) Leah may prepare the new will as long as it does not contain a substantial bequest to Leah.

(D) Leah must not permit Jacob to make a substantial bequest to her daughter.

23. Nancy Hall is an attorney who formerly represented Lisa Logan in connection with Logan's plans to develop a shopping center. Logan terminated Hall's representation when Logan decided to delay, but not cancel, the plans for the shopping center. The plans for the shopping center are still secret. Hall now has the opportunity to purchase land next to the proposed site of the center at an advantageous price, and she is tempted to do so because she knows that Logan will need the land for parking when she develops the shopping center. Which of the following statements most accurately describes Hall's options under the Model Rules of Professional Conduct?

(A) Hall may not purchase the land unless she obtains the informed consent of her former client.

(B) Hall may purchase the land because Logan terminated her services and forfeited any right to confidentiality of her plans.

(C) Hall may purchase the land as long as she first informs the seller of her former client's plans to develop the shopping center.

(D) Hall may purchase the land because Logan is a former client.

24. Diane Simmons is an attorney who represents Blake Jeffries, who has been accused of abducting a young woman who was hiking in a nearby national forest. Jeffries tells Simmons that he did abduct the girl, and the girl is presently tied up without food or water in a cabin deep in the forest. Which of the following statements most accurately states the lawyer's options?

   (A) The lawyer must reveal this information to save the girl.

   (B) The lawyer may choose not to reveal the information, in order to protect her client.

   (C) The lawyer may reveal the information only with her client's informed consent.

   (D) The lawyer must not reveal this information.

25. Randall Young is an attorney who specializes in commercial real estate transactions. One of Young's regular clients is about to close a sale of a property to an out-of-state buyer. Young is assisting his client with the transaction. The client now tells Young that, unbeknownst to the buyer, the property has been "flipped" several times in order to bring a higher sale price. Under the applicable law, the practice of "flipping" property without disclosing that it has occurred is fraud. Which of the following statements most accurately describes Young's options?

   (A) The lawyer must not assist with the transaction but must not reveal the fraud to the buyer.

   (B) The lawyer may assist with the transaction but has the option to tell the buyer about the fraud.

   (C) The lawyer may assist with the transaction and may not tell the buyer about the fraud.

   (D) The lawyer must not assist with the transaction.

26. A lawyer regularly represents plaintiffs in automobile accident cases. She represents Jeremiah McFarland and obtains a sizeable judgment for him, despite the assertion of a comparative negligence defense based upon allegations that Jeremiah habitually sends text messages while he drives. A year later, the lawyer is asked to represent a new plaintiff, this time for a car accident allegedly caused by Jeremiah, who will be the defendant. May the lawyer undertake the new representation?

ANSWER:

27. A lawyer agrees to represent an elderly husband (who has three children from an earlier marriage) and his new young wife in the creation of their wills and other documents related to their estate plans. The lawyer perceives that there is a significant risk of a material limitation in his representation of the wife because of the lawyer's duties to the husband, and vice versa (for example, the husband and wife may differ over disposition of any of his assets to his children). The lawyer reasonably believes that he can nevertheless provide competent and diligent representation to both clients. What must the lawyer do in order to proceed for both of them?

ANSWER:

28. Matt Hollis is an attorney who works as in-house counsel for a company that provides technical support for on-line video gaming. In the ordinary course of its business, the company acquires the credit card numbers of the players who use the company's services. Matt has just learned that one division of the company has been inflating its profitability figures by illegally selling the credit card numbers. When Matt confronted the manager of this division, the manager told Matt that she was not going to stop the practice and that Matt was instructed to keep it quiet. What is Matt's obligation under the Model Rules of Professional Conduct?

ANSWER:

29. Nina Majors is an attorney who has been representing five families who own lots on the same "resort lake." Nina has filed suit on behalf of each homeowner against the seller of the lots because, as it turns out, the lots flood on a regular basis. The seller has made a settlement offer to settle all five claims for a total of $250,000, with the amounts allocated to each plaintiff to be proportional to the size of the lot owned by that plaintiff. Under the Model Rules of Professional Conduct, what steps must Nina take with respect to the settlement?

ANSWER:

30. Sylvia Greco is an attorney who has been representing Millbank Food Stores, Inc. on a variety of matters, off and on, for many years. Sylvia has just completed her only pending matter for Millbank, and Sylvia has decided that she will not represent Millbank on any future matters. Is it necessary or advisable for Sylvia to affirmatively terminate her relationship with Millbank even though she no longer has any open files for the company? Why or why not?

ANSWER:

31. Donder, English, and Fredrickson (D E & F) is a large law firm that regularly seeks and obtains advance waivers of conflicts of interest from new clients. The firm recently obtained such an advance waiver from Stardust, Inc., when the firm agreed to represent Stardust in a multi-party lawsuit. Stardust is a sophisticated consumer of legal services and was independently represented when it entered into the advance waiver. Now a distant branch office of D E & F has been retained by a different client to assert a claim against Stardust in the same case for which Stardust initially hired D E & F. Is the advance waiver effective such that this representation by the branch office will be permitted?

ANSWER:

32. A lawyer specializes in defending cases in which the defendant is charged with driving under the influence. The lawyer receives a call from Osgood Slater, who asks the lawyer to represent

Osgood's son, who has just been charged with that crime. Osgood tells the lawyer that Osgood will pay for the representation. Under what circumstances, if any, may the lawyer undertake the representation of Osgood's son?

ANSWER:

33. Rene Hotchkiss is an attorney who currently represents the Allgood Insurance Company (AIC). She has been asked to represent a plaintiff in a lawsuit involving an automobile accident. The defendant's insurer is AIC, and this is not a "direct action" state. Rene's partner has told her that she absolutely cannot take this new case because she "cannot sue his own client." Rene thinks that *maybe* she can undertake this new representation. Who is right, Rene or her partner?

ANSWER:

34. Abby Peters is an attorney who regularly represents Herman Maris. Abby has now been asked by Herman's mother Nancy to re-draft Nancy's will to disinherit Herman. Such a step would be legal in their state, and Nancy does not want advice about whether to disinherit Herman — she just wants Abby to "draw it up." Does Abby have a conflict of interest?

ANSWER:

35. Sheila Allman is a lawyer who represents Peterman Huffington, IV. Huffington instructs Allman to draft him a new will and to leave all of his estate to his new wife. Sheila knows that making such a will would put Huffington in breach of his written contract to provide funds for the college educations of his children by his first wife, even in the event of his death. Which of the following statements most accurately describes Sheila's options under the Model Rules of Professional Conduct?

    (A) Sheila must refuse to assist her client because she would be assisting with a breach of contract.

    (B) Sheila must advise her client that the new will would be a breach of contract.

    (C) Sheila may draft the will and need not advise her client of the breach of contract.

    (D) Sheila must advise her client of the breach of contract but must draft the will if her client insists.

36. Matthew Hicks is an attorney who is defending Star Enterprises, Inc. (SEI) in a civil case in which SEI is accused of fraud. Meanwhile, SEI is applying to a local bank for an extension on its line of credit, and SEI has asked Hicks to prepare and deliver a written report to the bank about the transaction that was allegedly fraudulent. Which of the following statements most accurately describes the lawyer's options under the Model Rules of Professional Conduct?

    (A) Hicks may prepare and deliver the evaluation with the informed consent of his client.

    (B) Hicks may not perform the evaluation for the bank because doing so is incompatible with his role as advocate for SEI.

    (C) Hicks may perform and deliver the evaluation to the bank as long as the report does not affect SEI's interests materially and adversely.

    (D) Hicks may not prepare and deliver the evaluation to the bank because he would be revealing information relating to the representation of his client.

37. A lawyer has represented Monolith, Incorporated for a number of years. She receives a call from the general counsel for Monolith, an experienced attorney who is a highly sophisticated consumer of legal services. The general counsel asks the lawyer, "may we compensate an official of a foreign government for his consulting services in connection with our export of products into his country. Don't preach to me — I just want technical legal advice on that question." Which of the following statements most accurately reflects

the lawyer's options under the Model Rules of Professional Conduct?

(A) The lawyer may always give clients technical legal advice if the client is clear that this is all the client wants.

(B) The lawyer must not accept the question at face value but instead must probe the client's plan to see if more detailed advice is necessary.

(C) The lawyer must never give a client just technical legal advice.

(D) The lawyer may accept the request at face value and give just the technical legal advice requested.

38. Susan Richey is an attorney who specializes in prenuptial agreements. Her client, Barbara Clawson, is a divorced mother of two girls. Barbara is about to marry Jay Browning, a widowed father of two much younger boys. Barbara instructs Susan to write a prenuptial agreement that will require Jay to fund the girls' higher education fully (including graduate or professional school), regardless of the girls' other means and regardless of Jay's ability to provide for his boys. Which of the following statements most accurately describes Susan's options under the Model Rules of Professional Conduct?

(A) Susan may but need not counsel Barbara on the morality of such an agreement.

(B) Susan must counsel Barbara on the morality of such an agreement.

(C) Susan may not counsel Barbara on the morality of the agreement because moral advice is not part of the lawyer's role.

(D) Susan must decline to assist Barbara in making such an agreement.

39. Katie Gondorff is an attorney who has been asked by a client to undertake a title search and provide an opinion to third parties about the marketability of her client's property. Under the Model Rules of Professional Conduct, which of the following statements most accurately describes Katie's duties to the third parties?

(A) Katie has the same duties to the third parties that Katie would have to a client because Katie knows that the third parties are relying upon Katie's opinion.

(B) Katie's duties to third parties are governed by other law and not the Rules of Professional Conduct.

(C) Katie has only the duty not to make a false statement of material fact to the third parties.

(D) Katie has no duties to the third parties because they are not clients.

40. Fernando Ruiz is an attorney who is defending Roslyn Frisk on charges of drug trafficking. The judge in the case has just denied Fernando's motion to suppress the evidence against his client, and it appears that conviction, followed by a long prison term, is likely if the case goes to trial. The only alternative is for Roslyn to make a deal with the prosecution, testify against her friends, and seek a lighter sentence. Fernando knows that Roslyn will be distraught about this news and

will hate the idea of cooperating with the prosecution. What is Fernando's duty as a counselor to Roslyn?

ANSWER:

41. John Yau is an attorney who has been asked by his client, the owner of a rare book store, to give the client's bank a legal opinion that the client is in compliance with various loan covenants. As John proceeds with the investigation, it becomes clear that the client has no intention of cooperating and giving John all the documentation that John needs. It seems clear to John that if he presses for more information, he will be fired. Under the Model Rules of Professional Conduct, what advice should John give to his client about the legal opinion he will have to give under these circumstances?

ANSWER:

42. Cody Caldwell is an attorney who is representing the plaintiff in litigation over a breached contract. Under the applicable law, the plaintiff is entitled to recover reasonable attorney's fees as part of the remedy for the breach. Cody is the only person who can testify from personal knowledge about the hours spent on the case and the necessity for the work. Which of the following most accurately states Cody's options under the Model Rules of Professional Conduct?

   (A) Cody may testify about attorney's fees and still serve as his client's advocate.

   (B) Cody must withdraw from his role as advocate because he is a necessary witness in the case, but another lawyer in Cody's firm may act as advocate in the case for the client.

   (C) Cody must withdraw from his role as advocate because he is a necessary witness in the case, and no lawyer in Cody's firm may act as advocate for the plaintiff in the case.

   (D) Cody may not testify because he is the advocate for the plaintiff.

43. Emily Halpert is a criminal defense attorney. She recently held a press conference in which she told the press that one of her clients, Georgia Jackson, has been wrongfully accused of murder in the death of Georgia's boyfriend. Emily described the tests that her office had done on Georgia's car and stated that Georgia's car contained no fibers that matched the rug in which the boyfriend was wrapped when his body was found. Which of the following statements most accurately describes the propriety of Emily's statement under the Model Rules of Professional Conduct?

   (A) Emily's statement is permitted because it is protected by the First Amendment to the United States Constitution.

   (B) Emily's statement is permitted because it is within the "safe harbor" of permitted statements by defense counsel.

   (C) Emily's statement is not permitted because it relates to a case in which she represents one of the parties.

   (D) Emily's statement is not permitted because it reveals the result of a test on physical evidence in the case.

44. Dale Lambert is an attorney who represents Advanced Avionics, Inc. (AAI), a corporation that has been sued for defrauding the United States Government in connection with a contract to provide certain aircraft systems to the Air Force. Dale has just tracked down and interviewed a retired former employee of AAI, and this employee's testimony would

not be helpful to AAI. The former employee, however, is living on his pension from the company and is loyal to AAI's interests. The former employee has nothing to gain from talking to the lawyers for the plaintiff. Dale secures an agreement from the former employee not to speak informally with the lawyers for the plaintiff in the case. Which of the following statements most accurately describes the propriety of Dale's actions under the Model Rules of Professional Conduct?

(A) Dale violated the Rules because he asked a former employee not to talk to the plaintiff's lawyers.

(B) Dale violated the Rules because lawyers may not ask witnesses to refrain from voluntarily giving information to another party.

(C) Dale did not violate the Rules because the former employee's interests will not be adversely affected by refraining from giving information to plaintiff's counsel.

(D) Dale did not violate the Rules because the witness is a former employee of Dale's client.

45. Vickie Pickard is an attorney who is representing Earl Siebert in a criminal case. Earl wants Vickie to call his girlfriend as an alibi witness. Vickie does not know, but she reasonably suspects, that the girlfriend will be presenting false evidence. Which of the following statements most accurately describes Vickie's options under the Model Rules of Professional Conduct?

(A) Vickie must call the witness because she does not know that the testimony will be false, and her client has instructed her to call the witness.

(B) Vickie must withdraw from the case because to continue will require her to violate the Rules of Professional Conduct.

(C) Vickie has the option to call the witness or to refuse to call the witness.

(D) Vickie may not call the witness because Vickie reasonably believes that the witness will be presenting false evidence.

46. Deborah Laney is an attorney who is representing a client in a civil case. The case has gone well, and the parties are awaiting the jury's verdict. Deborah learns from her client that the opposing party in the case threatened a witness just before the witness testified on behalf of Deborah's client. To make such a threat is a crime in Deborah's jurisdiction. Which of the following statements most accurately describes Deborah's options under the Model Rules of Professional Conduct?

(A) Deborah must take reasonable remedial measures including, if necessary, disclosure of the threat to the tribunal.

(B) Deborah may disclose the threat to the tribunal only with the informed consent of her client because the making of the threat is information relating to the representation and thus is confidential.

(C) Deborah need not disclose the threat to the tribunal because it was made by someone other than her client or her client's agents.

(D) Deborah may but need not disclose the threat to the tribunal, since the witness apparently was not affected by the threat.

47. Amy Simon is an attorney whose client, Fred Birmingham, has been sued by his brother for exercising undue influence over his mother when his mother signed her last will and testament. Fred asks Amy whether it would be all right for him to destroy the letters that he exchanged with his mother during her last years because, he says, they are private and he does not want anyone to see them. With respect to advising Fred about the destruction of the letters, which of the following statements most accurately sets forth Amy's obligations under the Model Rules of Professional Conduct?

(A) Amy must not allow Fred to destroy the letters because they have potential evidentiary value.

(B) Amy must first determine if the destruction of the letters would be unlawful.

(C) Amy may allow Fred to destroy the letters as long as they have not been subpoenaed or requested by Fred's brother in the litigation.

(D) Amy may advise Fred that he has the right to destroy the letters but Amy must not personally participate in their destruction.

48. Sophie Wasserman is an attorney who, to her great surprise and disappointment, has just lost a jury trial. She wants to investigate whether there was juror misconduct that would give her a basis for a motion for new trial. As part of her investigation, Sophie wants to interview the jurors who served during her trial. Which of the following statements most accurately reflects Sophie's obligations under the Model Rules of Professional Conduct?

(A) The lawyer may communicate with the jurors unless doing so would violate a court rule or a court order.

(B) The lawyer may communicate with the jurors unless the communication would involve coercion, misrepresentation, duress, or harassment.

(C) The lawyer may not communicate with the jurors.

(D) The lawyer may not communicate with a juror who has made known to the lawyer a desire not to communicate with the lawyer.

49. Gerald Redmond is an attorney who has been asked by a client to file suit to have the state's Defense of Marriage Act (DOMA) held unconstitutional under the state's Constitution. Fifteen years ago, the state Supreme Court held squarely that the DOMA is constitutional under the state Constitution. Which of the following statements most accurately describes Gerald's options under the Model Rules of Professional Conduct?

(A) Gerald may file the case as long as he believes that he will prevail.

(B) Gerald may not file the case because it is frivolous.

(C) Gerald may file the case only if a reasonable attorney would conclude that there is a reasonable chance that the state Supreme Court will overturn the existing precedent.

(D) Gerald may file the case as long as he has a good faith argument to reverse the existing precedent.

50. Chad Timson is an attorney who has a case set for trial next week. Chad has just learned that his father is in the hospital with a serious infection. As it happens, Chad's client would benefit financially from a delay in the trial. Which of the following statements most accurately describes Chad's options under the Model Rules of Professional Conduct?

(A) Chad may not seek a continuance of the trial because his client will benefit financially from the delay.

(B) Chad may not seek to delay the trial because lawyers have an obligation to expedite litigation.

(C) Chad may seek continuance of the trial because he has a substantial purpose other than delay.

(D) Chad may seek continuance of the trial because doing so is consistent with the financial interests of the client.

51. Samuel Graham is an attorney who is in trial in a products liability case. During a break in the trial, he finds himself in an elevator with one of the jurors. Which of the following statements most accurately describes Samuel's obligations under the Model Rules of Professional Conduct?

(A) He may communicate with the juror as long as he limits his conversation to ordinary social pleasantries.

(B) He may communicate with the juror as long as he reports the conversation immediately to the court and his opposing party.

(C) He may communicate with the juror as long as the juror has not made known to the lawyer that she does not wish to communicate with him.

(D) He may not communicate with the juror unless he has been authorized by law or by court order to do so.

52. Justin Braswell is an attorney who is preparing to file a brief in opposition to a motion for summary judgment. Justin has located a case directly on point from his state's highest appellate court, the Supreme Court, but unfortunately the holding of the case is very harmful to Justin's arguments against summary judgment. Opposing counsel cited the case but did not realize how helpful it would have been to her motion. Which of the following statements most accurately describes Justin's options under the Model Rules of Professional Conduct?

(A) Justin need not cite the case because opposing counsel disclosed it.

(B) Justin must cite the case because it is directly on point.

(C) Justin must cite the case because it is from the highest appellate court in the state.

(D) Justin must not cite the case because it would violate his duty to be a zealous advocate for his client.

53. Glen Bogue is an attorney who is preparing his opening statement in a tort case that is about to go to trial. He wants to tell the jury about a theory of the case that will be supported by admissible evidence only if a test performed by his expert witness is deemed by the judge to be admissible. He is unsure whether the test will be admitted into evidence and therefore uncertain about whether to mention the conclusion it supports in his opening statement. Which of the following statements most accurately describes Glen's obligations under the Model Rules of Professional Conduct?

(A) Glen may mention the conclusion in his opening statement as long as he reasonably believes that the supporting evidence will be admitted.

(B) Glen may mention the conclusion in his opening statement as long as he has a good faith belief that the test will be admitted into evidence.

(C) Glen must not mention the conclusion in his opening statement unless he has obtained a prior ruling from the court that the supporting evidence will be admitted.

(D) Glen may mention the conclusion in his opening statement as long as he has a nonfrivolous argument for the admissibility of the supporting evidence.

54. Jane Peters is a prosecutor. Ten years ago, she obtained the conviction of Charles Storey for the rape and murder of a young girl. Jane has now received DNA test results that provide clear and convincing evidence that Charles is innocent of the crimes for which he was convicted. Which of the following statements most accurately describes Jane's obligations under the Model Rules of Professional Conduct?

(A) Jane has no obligation to do anything about the new evidence.

(B) Jane must seek to remedy the conviction.

(C) Jane must promptly disclose the evidence to the defendant and undertake further investigation.

(D) Jane must promptly disclose the evidence to the court in which the conviction was obtained.

55. Curt Gillespie is prosecuting Lucille Lemieux for the murder of Lucille's probation officer. The prosecution is seeking the death penalty. Curt has gathered unprivileged information during his investigation that shows what an unspeakably horrible childhood Lucille had. Curt knows that this information would be significant mitigation evidence at the sentencing phase of trial. Which of the following statements most accurately reflects Curt's options under the Model Rules of Professional Conduct?

(A) Curt must make timely disclosure of the evidence to the defense.

(B) Curt need not disclose the evidence to the defense because it does not relate to the defendant's guilt.

(C) Curt need not disclose the evidence to the defense because it is attorney work product.

(D) Curt must disclose the evidence to the defense if and when the defense requests it.

56. Stephen Carroll is an attorney who has just learned from a former client that the client lied at a court appearance in the client's case, which concluded a month ago. Which of the following statements most accurately describes Stephen's duties under the Model Rules of Professional Conduct?

(A) Stephen must seek to have the former client correct his testimony but, if that effort fails, inform the court that the former client lied.

(B) Stephen may not reveal the former client's false testimony because to do so would violate Benjamin's duty of confidentiality.

(C) Stephen must reveal the former client's false testimony because the former client perpetrated a fraud on the court.

(D) Stephen has no duty to reveal the former client's false testimony because the proceeding is concluded.

57. Shelley Henderson is an attorney who is representing her client at a deposition. The client testifies to something that Shelley knows is false. What duties, if any, does Shelley have because she knows her client is testifying to something that is false?

ANSWER:

58. Victor Stroman is a young associate at a law firm. His superior tells Victor to tell a prospective expert witness that, if the expert will testify for the firm's client and if the client wins, the firm will ask the expert to testify in numerous other similar cases. Under what circumstances, if any, may Victor do as instructed?

ANSWER:

59. Michelle Dumars is an attorney whose client has just delivered to her a gun that, the police believe, was used by the client to commit a murder. The client claims that he did not commit the murder. Michelle intends to turn the gun over to the police. Under the Model Rules of Professional Conduct, what should Michelle be concerned about before having the gun tested before turning it over to the police?

ANSWER:

60.   Linda Oliva is an attorney who represents a man whose son attempted suicide after the son was "cyber-bullied" on FaceBook. Linda intends to file a civil suit against the cyber-bullies to recover damages allegedly caused by their actions. No court in Linda's jurisdiction has ever considered whether there is a civil cause of action for "cyber-bullying." May Linda file this case, consistent with her responsibilities under the Model Rules of Professional Conduct?

ANSWER:

61.   Penny Lapp is an attorney who has just learned that her client changed the date on a crucial document in order to help defeat an argument that the client's claim is barred by the applicable statute of limitations. The document was admitted into evidence during the trial. The case has been submitted to the jury. What obligation, if any, does Penny have with respect to the falsified document?

ANSWER:

62. Rosemary Abel is an attorney who is representing the seller of an apartment complex. The client instructs Rosemary to tell the buyer's lawyer that "the complex is easily worth $2.5 million." In fact, the seller's latest appraisal indicates that the property is worth substantially less than that. Which of the following statements most accurately describes Rosemary's responsibilities under the Model Rules of Professional Conduct?

(A) Rosemary may not make the statement because it is a false statement of material fact.

(B) Rosemary may make the statement because she does not owe the other lawyer a duty of candor in an out-of-court negotiation.

(C) Rosemary may make the statement because it is not a statement of material fact.

(D) Rosemary may make the statement but must disclose the appraisal.

63. Clarence Widmer is an attorney who represents the Halcyon Property Company. His client is about to close a series of transactions with which Clarence is assisting. Clarence has just learned that his client fraudulently altered the inspection reports on the properties that it is selling, and upon which the buyers are relying. The client cannot be dissuaded from closing the transactions, and the buyers will suffer significant financial harm if the sales close. Which of the following statements most accurately states Clarence's responsibilities under the Model Rules of Professional Conduct?

(A) Clarence must withdraw from representing Halcyon and must inform the buyers of the fraud if disclosure is necessary to avoid assisting in the fraud.

(B) Clarence must withdraw from representing Halcyon but may not inform the buyers of the fraud because that information is confidential.

(C) Clarence must withdraw from representing Halcyon and may inform the buyers of the fraud if disclosure is necessary to avoid assisting in the fraud.

(D) Clarence may withdraw from representing Halcyon but may not inform the buyers of the fraud because that information is confidential.

64. Randy Pickett is an attorney who represents Wilco Paint Company. Wilco has been sued for employment discrimination by a woman who has been using her work e-mail account to send questions about the suit to and receive answers from her attorney. Under Wilco's written company policy, Wilco has the right to inspect and copy any messages sent or received on Wilco e-mail accounts. A Wilco executive copies the plaintiff's messages to and from her lawyer and sends those messages to Randy. Which of the following statements

most accurately describes Randy's duties under the Model Rules of Professional Conduct?

(A) Randy need not notify the plaintiff's attorney about these messages unless other law requires him to do so.

(B) Randy must notify the plaintiff's lawyer that Randy has possession of these messages.

(C) Randy must notify the plaintiff's lawyer that Randy has possession of these messages and send them to the plaintiff's lawyer.

(D) Randy must seek to withdraw from the case because he has used means of obtaining evidence that violate the rights of the plaintiff.

65. Ramon Martinez is an attorney who is representing a wife in a child custody dispute. Ramon receives an e-mail message from a woman who is a FaceBook "friend" of the husband. The e-mail message attaches a photo copied from the husband's FaceBook account in which the husband appears to be smoking marijuana. The friend attaches another in which the husband appears to be dancing nude on a beach with several other people in a similar state of undress. Ramon can reasonably assume that if he uses these photos at the custody hearing the husband will suffer serious embarrassment and perhaps lose his job as a counselor at a parochial school. Which of the following most accurately describes Ramon's options under the Model Rules of Professional Conduct?

(A) Ramon may use the photos because he did not obtain them illegally.

(B) Ramon may not use the photos because he would cause the husband embarrassment.

(C) Ramon may use the photos because he has a substantial purpose other than embarrassing the husband.

(D) Ramon may not use the photos unless his sole purpose in doing so is to demonstrate that his client should have custody of the children.

66. Brian Hubbard is an attorney who is eager to resolve a claim that is pending against his client in bankruptcy. Brian knows that the claim will not be dischargeable in bankruptcy as long as the claimant files a claim by the deadline. His opposing counsel is a young, inexperienced lawyer who knows little about the intricacies of bankruptcy law. Brian tells this young lawyer that if she files a claim it will just be discharged under bankruptcy law. Which of the following statements most accurately describes the propriety of this statement under the Model Rules of Professional Conduct?

(A) The statement is not misconduct because no reasonable lawyer would rely upon opposing counsel to accurately state the law that will apply to a dispute.

(B) The statement is not misconduct because it is not a false statement of material fact.

(C) The statement is misconduct because of the disparity in knowledge and experience between the two lawyers.

(D) The statement is misconduct because it is a false statement of law.

67. Victoria Shay is an attorney who is representing a class of plaintiffs against a large corporation in a case about the alleged manufacture and distribution of a defective drug. The drug company is of course represented by counsel, and Victoria knows that. A former employee of the company contacted Victoria, who secretly met with the former employee and obtained a large number of clearly privileged communications between the company's lawyers and senior company officials. Which of the following statements most accurately describes the propriety of Victoria's conduct under the Model Rules of Professional Conduct?

   (A) Victoria committed misconduct when she had direct contact with a former constituent of a represented party and when she obtained the privileged communications.

   (B) Victoria did not commit misconduct when she had direct contact with a former constituent of a represented party but did commit misconduct when she obtained the privileged communications.

   (C) Victoria committed misconduct when she had direct contact with a former constituent of a represented party but did not commit misconduct when she obtained the privileged communications.

   (D) Victoria did not commit misconduct.

68. Deanna Derosier is an attorney who is investigating a claim for a client about an accident on the property of Guillard Enterprises, Inc. (GEI). She has not filed the case yet, but she knows that GEI expects litigation and is represented by counsel in the matter. Deanna wants to speak to an employee of GEI without having to tell GEI's lawyer about the interviews. The employee works on GEI's loading dock and had nothing to do with the accident, except that the witness may have seen what happened when Deanna's client fell. Which of the following statements most accurately describes Deanna's options under the Model Rules of Professional Conduct?

   (A) Deanna may talk to the employee without notifying GEI's counsel as long as she does so before filing suit.

   (B) Deanna may not talk to the witness without notifying GEI's lawyer because Deanna knows that GEI is represented in the matter.

   (C) Deanna may talk to the witness without notifying GEI's counsel.

   (D) Deanna may not talk with the witness because the witness still works for GEI.

69. Lawrence Woolsey is an attorney who is handling a divorce case. Although the adverse party, Sandy Green, is represented by counsel, Lawrence has received a telephone call from Sandy to discuss the case with him. Which of the following statements most accurately describes Lawrence's options under the Model Rules of Professional Conduct?

   (A) Lawrence may continue the conversation as long as he informs Sandy's counsel immediately of the contact and discloses the substance of the conversations.

(B)   Lawrence may continue the conversation as long as he informs Sandy that he represents her husband and is therefore not disinterested.

(C)   Lawrence must terminate the conversation unless Sandy gives informed consent to speaking with him.

(D)   Lawrence must immediately terminate the conversation.

70.   Krista Waterman is an attorney whose client is about to have a meeting with the other party to a dispute. Krista wants the client to secretly record the conversation for Krista's use in connection with the dispute. Which of the following statements most accurately describes Krista's obligations under the Model Rules of Professional Conduct?

(A)   Krista may counsel the client to do the taping as long as doing so is legal in their jurisdiction.

(B)   Krista may counsel the client to tape the conversation because Krista is not personally participating in the taping.

(C)   Krista may not counsel the client to engage in the taping because she would be engaging in a criminal act that reflects adversely on her honesty and fitness as a lawyer in other respects.

(D)   Krista may not counsel the client to engage in the taping because she would be engaging in conduct involving dishonesty.

71.   Stanley Fredrickson is an attorney who for several years has been assisting a client in obtaining bank financing for new projects that use "fracking" to obtain oil and gas from rock formations. Stanley has several such deals underway for the client. Stanley has just learned that the client all along has been perpetrating an ongoing fraud with these deals. Which of the following statements most accurately describes Stanley's options under the Model Rules of Professional Conduct?

(A)   Stanley may immediately withdraw from the representation and may give notice of his withdrawal to the banks involved in the ongoing deals.

(B)   Stanley must immediately withdraw from the representation but may not under any circumstances give notice of his withdrawal to the banks involved in the ongoing deals.

(C)   Stanley may immediately withdraw from the representation but may not give notice of his withdrawal to the banks involved in the ongoing deals.

(D)   Stanley must immediately withdraw from the representation and may have to give notice of his withdrawal to the banks involved in the ongoing deals.

72.   Ralph Taggart is an attorney who is representing a client in a civil case involving an alleged breach of contract. A crucial issue in the case will be what the parties intended by certain provisions in their complicated contract. In discovery, Ralph has received an electronic version of the contract from her adversary's attorney. Ralph is informed that he can access certain "meta-data" in that contract, which may include revisions and comments that were made by the opposing party (and

not its counsel) during the negotiations over the contract. May Ralph take steps to access this "meta-data," consistent with his obligations under the Model Rules of Professional Conduct?

ANSWER:

73. Joy Conoway is an attorney who represents the wife in a divorce case. The husband is represented by counsel. Joy's client is tired of paying hefty legal bills and tired of seeing the marital estate dissipated by the similarly hefty legal bills that her husband is paying. Joy wants to suggest to her client that the client approach the husband directly about resolving all issues by agreement. Joy could coach her client on how to approach the husband and how best to negotiate a good deal. Is Joy's plan consistent with her responsibilities under the Model Rules of Professional Conduct?

ANSWER:

74. Dayle Ridley is an attorney who is in the midst of trying to negotiate the settlement of a civil claim with the assistance of a mediator. The mediator, who is not a judge, is conducting the settlement negotiations in a "caucus" format, and is shuttling back and forth between the parties. Ordinarily, Dayle would feel free in a negotiation to bluff about her settlement authority by telling the plaintiff's counsel that she cannot exceed a certain payment, even if her authority is actually for a greater amount. May Dayle engage in this tactic in a caucused mediation?

ANSWER:

75. Jack Harlow is an attorney who is moving from the only state where he is licensed to practice law. He has an offer in another state to go to work as in-house counsel for a major insurance company. Jack's job would be to counsel senior adjusters about how to make sure they avoid any "bad faith" claims and also to represent policyholders of the company in certain high profile cases in his new home state. May Jack undertake this new position, as described, consistent with his responsibilities under the Model Rules of Professional Conduct?

   (A) No, because Jack would be practicing law without a license in his new state.

   (B) No, because Jack would be appearing in court in his new state.

   (C) Yes, because Jack will be acting as in-house counsel.

   (D) Yes, because Jack is duly licensed in a U.S. jurisdiction.

76. Irene Wetmore is an attorney who is interested in joining a new firm in a metropolitan area. The firm has asked her to sign an employment agreement that states that, in exchange for the training the firm will provide, Irene will agree not to compete with the law firm for a period of one year in the metropolitan area. Which of the following statements most accurately reflects Irene's options under the Model Rules of Professional Conduct?

   (A) Irene may not agree to this provision.

   (B) Irene may agree to this provision as long as the restrictions of time and place are reasonable.

   (C) Irene may agree to this provision as long as she is receiving consideration for the agreement.

   (D) Irene may agree to this provision.

77. Carl Denton is an attorney who is employed full time by the Parents United to Protect Students (PUPS), a non-profit organization (controlled by nonlawyers) that provides legal representation in cases involving access to education for disabled people. Carl has just completed a case in which he was awarded $50,000 in attorney's fees under the Equal Access to Justice Act because he prevailed in an action against a local community college district. Which of the following statements most accurately describes Carl's options, with respect to the fees, under the Model Rules of Professional Conduct?

   (A) Carl may not share the fees with PUPS because the organization is controlled by nonlawyers.

(B) Carl may share the fees with PUPS because it is his employer and is a nonprofit organization.

(C) Carl may share the fees with PUPS because it is his employer.

(D) Carl may not share the fees with PUPS because the organization is not a law firm.

78. Laurie Traynor has a highly specialized practice. She is a leading expert on the standards that for-profit colleges must meet in order for their students to be eligible to receive federal student loans. She travels to many states and provides legal advice to institutions about compliance with these standards. She is licensed, however, only in one state. Which of the following statements most accurately describes the propriety of Laurie's practice under the Model Rules of Professional Conduct?

(A) Laurie's out-of-state activities violate the rule against practicing law in another jurisdiction without authority to do so.

(B) Laurie's out-of-state activities are permitted because she is giving advice about federal law.

(C) Laurie's out-of-state activities are permitted because they arise out of her home-state practice.

(D) Laurie's out-of-state activities are prohibited because she is not admitted pro hac vice in those states where she is not licensed.

79. Nick Kolb is an attorney who has decided that he no longer desires to keep up the pace required by a full-time solo practice. He does both estate planning and probate administration. Which of the following statements most accurately reflects Nick's options under the Model Rules of Professional Conduct?

(A) He may not sell the practice but may withdraw from representation of his clients because good cause exists to do so.

(B) He must sell his entire practice and retire if he chooses to sell any of it.

(C) He may sell the estate planning portion of his practice but remain in the practice of law part-time by maintaining his probate administration practice.

(D) He may sell a substantial portion of his practice if he gives reasonable notice to the affected clients.

80. Dane Finley is an attorney who recently won a major case. As soon as the verdict was announced, Dane's nonlawyer secretary sent the following message via Twitter: "Dane won big again. He can win big 4 u 2!" Dane soon found out about the message. Assuming that this was a false or misleading communication about Dane's services, under what circumstances, if any, will Dane will responsible for this violation of the Rules of Professional Conduct?

(A) Dane will not be responsible because he did not send the message.

(B)   Dane will not be responsible because he did not order his secretary to send the message.

(C)   Dane will not be responsible because he has done nothing to ratify the conduct.

(D)   Dane will be responsible unless he takes reasonable remedial action to avoid the consequences of the misconduct.

81.   Doug Oyler is an estate planning attorney who is licensed in a state that adjoins another state. To make ends meet, Doug regularly goes into the adjoining state to meet with clients and prepare their estate plans. He does not maintain an office in the adjoining state, and he is careful always to let his clients in that state know where he is licensed. Which of the following statements most accurately describes the propriety of Doug's actions under the Model Rules of Professional Conduct?

(A)   Doug is not committing misconduct because he has not established an office in the adjoining state.

(B)   Doug is not committing misconduct because he advises his clients truthfully about his licensure only in his home state.

(C)   Doug is committing misconduct by practicing law in a state where he is not licensed.

(D)   Doug is committing misconduct by continuous and systematic presence in the adjoining state for the practice of law.

82.   Harry Sherrill is an attorney who has been asked to litigate a case in a state that adjoins the only state in which he is licensed. He believes that there are witness interviews that must be conducted in that state. Which of the following statements most accurately describes Harry's options under the Model Rules of Professional Conduct?

(A)   Harry may conduct the interviews because doing so is a temporary activity and not the continuous and systematic practice of law in a state where he is not licensed.

(B)   Harry must not conduct the interviews until he is admitted pro hac vice in the case.

(C)   Harry can conduct the interviews before the case is filed because this activity is reasonably related to his practice in his home state.

(D)   Harry may conduct the interviews as long as he reasonably expects to be admitted pro hac vice in the case once it is filed.

83.   Amber Burris is an attorney who represents Paul Bunyan Insurance (PBI) in connection with the settlement of a class action lawsuit against PBI involving the sale of credit life insurance for new car buyers. PBI is so bitter about being sued that it instructs Amber to make the settlement offer but condition it on agreement by plaintiff's counsel never to sue PBI again for any client or class of clients. Which of the following statements best describes Amber's options under the Model Rules of Professional Conduct?

(A)   Amber may make the offer.

(B)   Amber must communicate to the client that she is not permitted by the Rules of Professional Conduct to make that offer.

(C)   Amber must immediately withdraw from representing PBI.

(D)   Amber must consult with the client about whether this offer is the best means of achieving the client's objectives.

84.   Keith Lopes is an attorney who is licensed in only one state. Keith is a tax lawyer. He prepares corporate and partnership tax returns. He does no litigation or alternative dispute resolution. He likes it that way. He receives a telephone call from his elderly Aunt Lucille in the distant state where Keith grew up. Aunt Lucille helped pay Keith's way through law school, and now she is asking for his help. She has been sued by a credit card company, and the court has ordered mediation. Aunt Lucille wants Keith to come home and represent her at the mediation. Which of the following statements most accurately describes Keith's options under the Model Rules of Professional Conduct?

(A)   Keith may represent Aunt Lucille because it would be a temporary activity related to an alternative dispute resolution proceeding.

(B)   Keith may represent Aunt Lucille only if he associates a lawyer licensed in her jurisdiction and that lawyer actively participates in the matter.

(C)   Keith may not represent Aunt Lucille because the mediation does not arise out of or reasonably relate to his practice.

(D)   Keith may not represent Aunt Lucille because he is not licensed in her jurisdiction.

85.   Melody Faulk is an attorney who frequently is appointed by her local court to represent indigent criminal defendants. In fact, the frequency of the appointments has become so great that she now believes she has as many cases as she can competently and diligently handle. The court contacts her about an additional appointment. What is her responsibility under the Model Rules of Professional Conduct?

ANSWER:

86.   Rita Hornbeck is an attorney who has received notice that the judge of her local criminal court intends to appoint Rita to represent the defendant in a murder case. When Rita arrives for the first hearing, she learns for the first time that the victim of the alleged murder was a former client of Rita. Is there any basis upon which Rita could seek to avoid the appointment as counsel in the murder case?

ANSWER:

87.   Ridgeway & Secrest (R & S) is a law firm that is concerned about departing partners who then take clients of the firm and otherwise compete with the firm. R & S is considering whether it can implement a "retirement plan" that would pay departing lawyers the amounts in their capital

accounts (which under the partnership agreement belong to the individual lawyers) and any fees earned by but not paid to the departing lawyers only on the condition that the departing lawyers not compete with R & S after their departure. Is the plan consistent with the Model Rules of Professional Conduct?

ANSWER:

88.   Penny Moss is an attorney who has been offered a job as an attorney for Costco Stores, Inc. Although Penny would be paid a salary by Costco, her clients would be individuals who are members of Costco's "Saver's Club," a membership that entitles members to shop at Costco stores and purchase household items in bulk, and which now includes the right to two hours per year of legal services provided by Costco lawyers. What concerns should Penny have about potential violations of the Model Rules of Professional Conduct if she accepts this position, given that she would be working as a salaried lawyer for Costco?

ANSWER:

89.   Reggie Grimes is an associate in the law firm of Winthorp & Winthorp. Reggie was admitted to the bar just a few months ago. Reggie has been instructed by one of the partners in his firm to file a lawsuit for a client and obtain an ex parte temporary restraining order to prevent a foreclosure sale of the client's property. The partner has instructed Reggie not to inform the court at the ex parte hearing of certain material facts that harm their client's case. Under the Model Rules of Professional Conduct, may Reggie follow the partner's instructions?

ANSWER:

90. Louise Runyon is an attorney who has just received notice that she has been appointed to represent an indigent criminal defendant. She will be paid a fraction of her usual hourly rate for this work and wishes to avoid having to do it. Which of the following statements is most likely under the Model Rules of Professional Conduct to allow her to seek to avoid the appointment?

    (A) "I am philosophically opposed to requiring lawyers to do pro bono service."

    (B) "This case will impose a financial burden on me."

    (C) "I am not competent to represent a criminal defendant."

    (D) "I am staunchly in favor of law and order and take a dim view of criminals."

91. Miriam Ackerman is an attorney who is a leading expert in the defense of prosecutions for driving under the influence of alcohol or drugs. Miriam is asked by a prospective client to represent him in such a case. The prospective client referred to Miriam in their meeting as "little lady." Which of the following statements most accurately sets forth Miriam's options under the Model Rules of Professional Conduct?

    (A) Miriam can decline the representation.

    (B) Miriam can decline the representation for good cause.

    (C) Miriam can decline the representation if the client's comment irritated her so much that the attorney-client relationship will be impaired.

    (D) Miriam cannot decline the representation.

92. Naomi Stine is a young, idealistic associate at a large commercial law firm. She wishes to convince the management committee of the firm to require all the lawyers in the firm to render pro bono service as a condition of continued employment. Under the Model Rules of Professional Conduct, which of the following persuasive statements could Naomi truthfully make?

    (A) Pro bono hours are required of every lawyer.

    (B) Fifty pro bono hours are required of every lawyer every year.

    (C) Every lawyer has a professional responsibility to provide legal services to those unable to pay.

(D) Every lawyer must either render 50 hours of pro bono service or make a financial contribution to an organization that provides legal services to persons of limited means.

93. Eugene Carmack is an attorney who is both a partner in a large urban law firm and a member of the Board of Directors of Eagle Legal Services, a local organization that renders service to people who cannot afford lawyers. Eagle has been asked to help some local residents sue Metropolitan Hospital for "patient dumping," a practice in which the hospital allegedly delivers non-critical, indigent patients in poor parts of town and abandons them there. Eugene's law firm represents Metropolitan Hospital in other matters. Under the Model Rules of Professional Conduct, which of the following statements most accurately reflects Eugene's options?

(A) Eugene must resign from the Board of Eagle Legal Services because he has a conflict of interest.

(B) Eugene must not participate in any decision of Eagle regarding the patient dumping litigation.

(C) Eugene may remain on the Board of Eagle Legal Services and participate in decisions regarding the patient dumping litigation because he is rendering pro bono service to the community.

(D) Eugene must avoid the potential conflict of interest either by ensuring that his firm does not represent Metropolitan Hospital in this matter or by resigning from the Eagle Board of Directors.

94. Joshua Sands is an attorney who just obtained a certification as a specialist in "Therapeutic Lawyering" from the Moon Beam Institute of Therapeutic Justice. The Institute has not yet been accredited or approved to grant specialist certifications by any state's authority or the American Bar Association. Joshua hopes that this new training and credential will help him attract the right kind of client. Which of the following statements most accurately describes Joshua's options under the Model Rules of Professional Conduct?

   (A) Joshua may advertise that he practices therapeutic law.

   (B) Joshua may advertise the certification because he actually acquired it.

   (C) Joshua may advertise the certification as long as he identifies the Institute as the organization that granted it.

   (D) Joshua may advertise the certification as long as his advertisement is not false or misleading.

95. Wayne Youngblood is an attorney who wants to attract business in the following way. He has a friend who works for a chiropractor. Wayne wants to make an agreement with the friend under which Wayne will hire the friend for $1000 to write an advertisement for Wayne every time the friend sends a patient to Wayne and that patient signs up as a client with Wayne. Which of the following most accurately describes the propriety of Wayne's plan under the Model Rules of Professional Conduct?

   (A) Wayne may not execute this plan because he may not give anyone anything of value in exchange for recommending his services.

   (B) Wayne may not execute this plan without the informed consent of the clients he obtains this way.

   (C) Wayne may execute the plan because he is permitted to pay for advertising services.

   (D) Wayne may execute the plan as long as the referral arrangement is not exclusive.

96. Cathy Rodriguez is an attorney whose specialty is civil rights litigation. Cathy learns that several students have been suspended from an elite local private high school for wearing shirts with slogans that denounce war. She wants to represent these students to establish important precedent but she also needs the money that the wealthy parents of the students could afford to pay. Which of the following statements most accurately describes Cathy's options under the Model Rules of Professional Conduct?

(A) Cathy may solicit the students because she is not motivated entirely by pecuniary gain.

(B) Cathy may solicit the students because this is a civil rights case.

(C) Cathy may not solicit the students because pecuniary gain is a significant motive for doing so.

(D) Cathy may not solicit the students because they are not existing clients.

97. Scott Clough is an attorney who wants to advertise that he was honorary chairman of the local judge's recent successful reelection campaign. Which of the following statements most accurately describes Scott's obligations under the Model Rules of Professional Conduct?

(A) Scott may not use the advertisement because it is in poor taste.

(B) Scott may not use this advertisement because it implies an ability to achieve results by means that would violate the law.

(C) Scott may use the advertisement if he obtains the judge's permission to do so.

(D) Scott may use this advertisement if it is true.

98. Judy Meade is an attorney whose specialty is estate planning. Judy also volunteers for the local softball league, and in that capacity she has come into possession of the cell phone numbers of all the parents of players in the league. These parents are exactly the type of clients that Judy would like to have, and she has recently learned how to send text messages with her cell phone. Judy would like to send a text message to all the parents on the list and offer her services as an attorney. A few of the parents are Judy's close personal friends, but the rest are not. Which of the following statements most accurately describes Judy's options under the Model Rules of Professional Conduct?

(A) Judy may send the message as long as it is not false or misleading.

(B) Judy may send the message only to the parents who are close personal friends.

(C) Judy may not send the message unless she includes the words, "Advertising Material" at the beginning and end of the message to all recipients other than close personal friends.

(D) Judy may not send the message because it would be improper solicitation.

99. Robert Katz is an attorney whose firm specializes in receiverships of financial institutions. Frank has received a request from the Federal Deposit Insurance Corporation that asks his firm to submit a written proposal to represent the FDIC in a certain region for a certain period of time. Which of the following statements most accurately reflects Robert's options under the Model Rules of Professional Conduct?

(A) Robert may submit the written proposal.

(B) Robert may submit the written proposal as long as it contains the words "advertising material" on the outside of the envelope.

(C) Robert may not submit the proposal unless he has a prior professional relationship with the FDIC.

(D) Robert may not submit the proposal if pecuniary gain is a significant motivation.

100. Joe Lemire is an attorney who is attempting to establish his practice in his hometown of Centerville. He believes that it would help him do so to advertise his practice as the "Centerville Legal Clinic." Which of the following statements most accurately describes Joe's obligations under the Model Rules of Professional Conduct?

(A) Joe may use the trade name if he includes a disclaimer that makes it clear that his practice is not a public legal aid agency.

(B) Joe may use the trade name as long as its offices are located in Centerville.

(C) Joe may not practice law using a trade name.

(D) Joe may use the trade name as long as the practice specializes in providing legal services to low-income clients.

101. Clarence & Madsen is a law firm that has applied to become the contract public defender for the county. Under the contract, the county would pay the firm $20,000 per month in exchange for which the firm would represent all of the county's indigent criminal defendants. The contract is awarded by the chief judge of the state court. In the past election cycle, the firm contributed a significant amount of money to the reelection campaign of the chief judge. Which of the following statements most accurately describes the firm's options under the Model Rules of Professional Conduct?

(A) The firm may not accept the contract because it made campaign contributions to the chief judge.

(B) The firm may not accept the contract if it made the contributions for the purpose of obtaining or being considered for the contract.

(C) The firm may accept the contract as long as the campaign contributions would not constitute bribery or another crime.

(D) The firm may accept the contract.

102. Aaron Chapman and Brian McCain are attorneys who were law school classmates. They have entered into an office-sharing arrangement under which they share rent for office space and share the costs of common areas and services such as a secretary and a copier. Each will retain control over his own cases, billing, and revenue. To garner greater credibility for their respective practices, and to save money on letterhead, they want to practice under the name "Chapman & McCain." Under the Model Rules of Professional Conduct, which of the following statements most accurately reflects the lawyers' options?

(A) The lawyers may describe themselves as Chapman & McCain because they share office space.

(B)   The lawyers may describe themselves as Chapman & McCain because those are their real names.

(C)   The lawyers may not describe themselves as Chapman & McCain because they are not members of the same law firm.

(D)   The lawyers may not describe themselves as Chapman & McCain unless they inform all prospective clients that they do not practice as a law firm.

103.   Jesse Compton is an attorney who is considering whether he should participate in a prepaid legal services plan owned and operated by a national company. He is concerned because he knows that employees of the plan personally contact people and ask them to become members. Under the Model Rules of Professional Conduct, which of the following statements most accurately describes the propriety of Jesse's participation in the plan?

(A)   Jesse may participate in the plan as long as the prospective members being contacted are not known to be in need of particular services covered by the plan.

(B)   Jesse may not participate because the plan is engaged in improper solicitation of prospective clients.

(C)   Jesse may participate in the plan because he does not own the plan or direct its activities.

(D)   Jesse may participate because he is not personally soliciting prospective clients.

104.   Antonio Vitale is an attorney who wants to increase the volume of new clients served by his law firm, which specialize in representing people who have been involved in automobile accidents. Antonio wants to sign a contract to pay a local, non-profit referral service for including him on its roster of attorneys. Under the Model Rules of Professional Conduct, which of the following statements most accurately describes the propriety of Antonio's plan?

(A)   Antonio may pay the referral service if the service has been approved by his state's regulatory authority.

(B)   Antonio may pay the referral service as long as he is only paying its usual charges for inclusion on the list.

(C)   Antonio may not pay the referral service.

(D)   Antonio may pay the referral service because he does not own or operate it himself.

105.   Mary Jane McCorkle is an attorney who specializes in personal injury cases for plaintiffs. Mary Jane has a cousin, Gretchen, to whom she is very close. Gretchen's husband Patrick is a corporate lawyer who was recently injured in a collision with a gravel truck. Mary Jane wants to contact Patrick, whom she does not know, by telephone and offer to represent him for her usual fee. Under the Model Rules of Professional Conduct, which of the following statements most accurately describes the propriety of Mary Jane's proposed course of conduct?

(A) Mary Jane may not call Patrick because she is motivated by pecuniary gain.

(B) Mary Jane may not call Patrick because she does not know him and has never represented him.

(C) Mary Jane may call Patrick because she has a close family relationship with Patrick's wife.

(D) Mary Jane may call Patrick because he is a lawyer.

106. William Broughton is an attorney who recently paid AMERILAW, a trade publication, to be included in the publication's list of "Best Lawyers in America." Under the Model Rules of Professional Conduct, which of the following statements most accurately describes William's options regarding publication of this honor?

(A) William may advertise himself as one of the "AMERILAW Best Lawyers in America" because it is true that he was on the list.

(B) William may advertise himself as one of the "AMERILAW Best Lawyers in America" because he has a constitutional right to advertise.

(C) William may not advertise himself as one of the "AMERILAW Best Lawyers in America" because the statement would be misleading.

(D) William may not advertise himself as one of the "AMERILAW Best Lawyers in America" because it is an implied comparison with other lawyers' services.

107. Gustav Spillers is an attorney who wants to be known as the kind of lawyer who will "go the extra mile for a client." He actually does violate the law and rules of conduct when it is necessary to help his clients. Gustav proposes to run an advertisement that shows a poker player holding a hand of five aces, with the caption, "You need a lawyer who knows how to stack the deck. Call Gustav Spillers at 1-800-CHEATER." Under the Model Rules of Professional Conduct, which of the following statements most accurately describes the propriety of Gustav's advertisement?

(A) The advertisement is permissible because questions of taste are matters of speculation and subjective judgment.

(B) The advertisement is permissible because it is not false or misleading.

(C) The advertisement is impermissible because it brings disrepute to the legal profession and the system of justice.

(D) The advertisement is impermissible because it implies that Gustav can achieve results by violating the rules of conduct or other law.

108. Sonny Guest is an attorney who wishes to advertise using the following slogans: "When you need a lawyer, save money by seeing Sonny" and "For your legal needs, Guest is the best!" What advice would you give Sonny about the propriety of these advertisements under the Model Rules of Professional Conduct?

ANSWER:

109. Hattie Dougherty is an attorney who specializes in representing plaintiffs in accidents involving all-terrain vehicles. She has won several huge verdicts that have garnered headlines such as "Hattie Wins $10 million Verdict from Local Jury" and "Dougherty Does it Again: ATV Manufacturer Socked for $15.2 million." Hattie would like to include a "montage" of these headlines as the background for her new television advertisements. What advice would you give Hattie about the propriety of this idea under the Model Rules of Professional Conduct?

ANSWER:

110. Rita McCue is an attorney who specializes in elder law. She would like to increase her volume of business by conducting a series of "educational seminars" around her state through the auspices of local senior citizen centers. She is hoping that many of the attendees will become clients. As she embarks on his tour of seminars, what ethical advice would you give Rita?

ANSWER:

111. Raymond Palermo is an attorney in a small town. He has recently been disturbed by the behavior of one of his fellow lawyers, Marvin Tobias. Raymond has noticed that Marvin has repeatedly missed deadlines in cases they have together, and Marvin also failed to appear on time for the last two status conferences they were to have with the court. Yesterday, Marvin appeared in court with Raymond, but Marvin appeared to be intoxicated. Raymond smelled alcohol on Marvin's breath before the hearing. This is not the first time recently when Raymond has seen Marvin intoxicated at the courthouse. Which of the following statements most accurately states Raymond's responsibilities under the Model Rules of Professional Conduct?

    (A) Raymond may report Marvin's apparent impairment to the appropriate professional authorities because it raises a substantial question as to his fitness to practice law.

    (B) Raymond must report Marvin's apparent impairment to the appropriate professional authorities because Marvin's failure to withdraw from representing his clients raises a substantial question as to his fitness to practice law.

    (C) Raymond may not report Marvin's apparent impairment to the appropriate professional authorities because Marvin has not violated a rule of professional conduct.

    (D) Raymond need not report Marvin's apparent impairment to the appropriate professional authorities if Raymond reports it to an approved lawyers assistance program.

112. Professor April Cameron is a member of the bar but does not practice law. The dean of her law school, Albert Morey, is also a non-practicing member of the same bar. April has learned that Dean Morey has been embezzling law school funds, which is a crime in their jurisdiction. Although April believes that the matter can be handled quietly within the law school, she is considering whether she must report Dean Morey to the appropriate professional authorities. Which of the following statements most accurately states April's responsibilities under the Model Rules of Professional Conduct?

    (A) April need not report Dean Morey's conduct because the commission of a crime unrelated to the practice of law is not misconduct under the Rules of Professional Conduct.

    (B) April need not report Dean Morey's conduct because he does not practice law.

    (C) April need not report Dean Morey's conduct because she is a non-practicing lawyer.

    (D) April must report Dean Morey's conduct because his criminal activity is a violation of the Rules of Professional Conduct that reflects adversely on his honesty, trustworthiness, or fitness as a lawyer.

113. Bryan Wilkins is an attorney who is representing a client in a civil lawsuit against the client's former business partner. During the discovery process, Bryan receives evidence from an anonymous source that his opposing counsel, Cassandra Leonard, deliberately destroyed important discoverable evidence. Such an act is criminal obstruction of justice in their state. Bryan is disturbed by this but is about to settle the case and fears taking any action that would disrupt the settlement. Which of the following statements most accurately describes Bryan's options under the Model Rules of Professional Conduct?

    (A) Bryan must report Cassandra's misconduct to the bar because it is a violation of the rules that reflects adversely on her honesty, trustworthiness, or fitness as a lawyer.

    (B) Bryan may but need not report Cassandra's misconduct to the bar because it is a violation of the rules that reflects adversely on her honesty, trustworthiness, or fitness as a lawyer.

    (C) Bryan may not report Cassandra's misconduct to the bar because it is information relating to the representation of his client.

    (D) Bryan may report Cassandra's misconduct to the bar only if he obtains his client's informed consent to do so.

114. Kayla Goodman is an attorney who ran an unsuccessful race to unseat an incumbent trial judge. As part of her campaign efforts, Kayla solicited campaign contributions from fellow lawyers and from leading business leaders in the community. Which of the following statements most accurately describes the propriety of Kayla's conduct?

    (A) Kayla violated both the Model Code of Judicial Conduct and the Model Rules of Professional Conduct.

    (B) Kayla violated the Model Code of Judicial Conduct.

    (C) Kayla violated the Model Rules of Professional Conduct.

    (D) Kayla did not violate any rules of conduct.

115. Adam Collins is an attorney who tried without success to destroy evidence in a bitter divorce case. Adam "erased" and "deleted" a number of incriminating e-mails that his client had sent, for the purpose of making sure that those messages would not be available to her husband at trial. Unbeknownst to Adam, however, it is extremely difficult to "erase" e-mail, and a forensic computer specialist was able to retrieve the messages and testify about Adam's amateurish attempts to "destroy" them. Because he failed, Adam did not violate the state obstruction of justice statute. Which of the following statements most accurately describes the propriety of Adam's conduct under the Model Rules of Professional Conduct?

    (A) Adam did not commit misconduct because he failed to destroy the evidence.

    (B) Adam did not commit misconduct because he did not commit a crime.

    (C) Adam committed misconduct because he attempted to violate a rule of professional conduct.

(D) Adam committed misconduct because he attempted to commit a criminal act that would have reflected adversely on his honesty, trustworthiness, or fitness as a lawyer.

116. Diana Kelley is an attorney who recently went into a state adjacent to the state where she is licensed and, while she was providing temporary legal services there, engaged in actions that constitute misconduct in both states. Assume that both states have adopted the Model Rules of Professional Conduct. Under the Model Rules of Professional Conduct, in which state or states is Diana subject to discipline?

   (A) Diana is subject to discipline in both states.

   (B) Diana is subject to discipline only in the state where the conduct occurred.

   (C) Diana is subject to discipline only in the state where the predominant effect of the misconduct occurred.

   (D) Diana is subject to discipline only in the state where he is licensed.

117. Sean is an attorney who has just received a speeding ticket while he was driving to the courthouse to try to file a complaint before the clerk's office closed on the last day before the statute of limitations would run on his client's claim. Under the Model Rules of Professional Conduct, which of the following statements most accurately describes Sean's situation?

   (A) Sean did not commit misconduct because a speeding ticket does not reflect adversely on his honesty, truthfulness, or fitness as a lawyer.

   (B) Sean committed misconduct by violating the law while he was acting as a lawyer.

   (C) Sean did not commit misconduct because the Rules of Professional Conduct do not regulate how a lawyer drives.

   (D) Sean committed misconduct by showing disrespect for the law.

118. Ellen Wagner is a lawyer whose former law partner began several years ago to display signs of senile dementia. As the symptoms grew worse, the firm instituted policies and procedures to make sure that no client matters were neglected, and Ellen believes that those procedures were successful. Ellen's partner has now left the firm and opened his own law office. Ellen has no reason to believe that the safeguards the firm had in place will be in place at the departing lawyer's new office. Several of Ellen's clients have discharged Ellen and retained her former partner instead. Ellen fears that his deteriorating mental condition will cause harm to those former clients. Must Ellen tell them about the problem?

ANSWER:

119. Clara Bailey is an attorney in a case about mortgage fraud. She learns that her opposing counsel assisted the opposing party in the fraud and would like to threaten to reveal that information to the bar during negotiations to resolve the case. Under the Model Rules of Professional Conduct,

would it be a permissible negotiation strategy to threaten to reveal to the bar the other lawyer's assistance in a fraud?

ANSWER:

120. Professor Richard Morris has long had aspirations to be an appellate judge. He learns that his rival on the faculty, Edward Curran, is being considered for appointment to the court of appeals. Richard receives a call from the newspaper, and is asked about Edward's judicial temperament. Under the Model Rules of Professional Conduct, what constraints are there on what Richard may say about Edward?

ANSWER:

121. Judge Otis Newton's family has owned a dry cleaner's store for three generations. His parents have retired, and the judge's sister cannot run the business entirely on her own. The business is in the judge's hometown, which is in another judicial circuit. His sister has asked the judge to co-manage the business with her. Which of the following statements most accurately describes the judge's options under the Model Code of Judicial Conduct?

    (A) The judge may not become a co-manager of any business while he holds judicial office.

    (B) The judge may become a co-manager of the business because it operates in another judicial circuit.

    (C) The judge may become a co-manager of the business unless doing so would interfere with the proper performance of judicial duties.

    (D) The judge may become a co-manager of the business because it is a business that is closely held by members of the judge's family.

122. Judge Stacey Mulligan has been assigned a criminal case in which the defendant is accused of shoplifting a loaf of bread to eat. Because the defendant has been convicted of previous crimes, the defendant is subject to a long mandatory "three-strikes" sentence if he is convicted. That sentence seems grossly unfair to Judge Mulligan under the circumstances. The judge nevertheless can be fair to both sides, and because she has told no one of her feelings about the law, her impartiality could not reasonably be questioned. Which of the following statements most accurately describes Judge Mulligan's obligations under the Model Code of Judicial Conduct?

    (A) The judge must recuse herself because of her strong feelings about the law.

    (B) The judge must do substantial justice regardless of the letter of the law.

    (C) The judge must apply the law without regard to the judge's disapproval of the law.

    (D) The judge may recuse herself because of her strong feelings about the law.

123. Judge Ronald Bennett recently presided over a bench trial concerning a business dispute between two men who, the evidence showed, had at one time been both business partners and domestic partners. During the course of the trial, the judge referred to the parties as "these two gay guys who couldn't get along" and stated that "these two homosexuals should have left their spats at home and not taken them to the office." Which of the following statements most accurately describes the propriety of these statements under the Model Code of Judicial Conduct?

(A) The remarks are inappropriate statements of bias or prejudice regarding the parties' sexual orientation.

(B) The remarks are not inappropriate, because the Model Code of Judicial Conduct does not prohibit manifestations of bias regarding sexual orientation.

(C) The remarks are not inappropriate, because they are relevant to the matter in dispute.

(D) The remarks are not inappropriate, because the parties' sexual orientation was part of the evidence in the case.

124. Judge Steven Young is new to the bench and ambitious to put into place what he calls his "rocket docket." As part of this plan, Judge Young intends to require and personally oversee settlement negotiations in all of his civil cases and plea negotiations in all of his criminal cases. Under the Model Code of Judicial Conduct, which of the following statements best describes the propriety of Judge Young's plan?

(A) The plan is permissible as long as the judge does not coerce settlements or pleas.

(B) The plan is permissible for cases that will go to jury trial if there is no pre-trial resolution but not for ones that will go to bench trials.

(C) The plan is permissible for civil cases but not for criminal cases.

(D) The plan is impermissible because of the judge's personal involvement in negotiations.

125. Judge Terri Alexander is a new judge who is eager to learn everything she can about the inner workings of the judicial process. She is also very interested in getting reelected to her job. Judge Alexander is considering a new policy for her court. The plan is that, after every jury trial, the judge will invite the jurors to join her in the jury room for coffee and a "focus group" discussion of the jurors' experience. Which of the following statements is the best advice for Judge Alexander about implementing this plan consistent with her obligations under the Model Code of Judicial Conduct?

(A) The judge may conduct the focus groups as long as she does not commend or criticize what the jury decided in the particular case.

(B) The judge may conduct the focus groups as long as she does not discuss the merits of the case or the verdict.

(C) The judge may not conduct the focus groups unless all parties to the case are permitted to attend.

(D) The judge may not conduct the focus groups.

126. Judge Colleen Ward is presiding over a trade secret case involving algorithms used in programming devices that use artificial intelligence. The judge does not understand how she is supposed to go about ruling on the admissibility of some of the scientific evidence in the case. She calls the judge she replaced (he is now in private practice) and gets guidance from him about how to handle that evidence. With that background, the judge holds the

preliminary hearing and then explains her tentative ruling. The judge explains the basis for her ruling and describes the guidance she received from the former judge and invites further comments and arguments from counsel. Which of the following most accurately describes the propriety of the judge's conduct under the Model Code of Judicial Conduct?

(A) The judge violated the Code of Judicial Conduct because she obtained the advice of a disinterested expert on the law.

(B) The judge violated the Code of Judicial Conduct because she obtained the advice of a disinterested expert on the law without prior written notice to the parties.

(C) The judge did not violate the Code of Judicial Conduct because the expert she consulted was disinterested.

(D) The judge did not violate the Code of Judicial Conduct because she gave the parties the opportunity to respond to the advice she received from the former judge.

127. Judge Reginald McCarthy recently decided a difficult discovery issue in a civil case. He ruled that the Attorney General of his state could not discover records relating to the identities of women who obtained abortions at a local hospital. The Attorney General has applied for a writ of mandamus, and the case is receiving an enormous amount of media attention. Although there have been no allegations concerning his conduct in the matter, Judge McCarthy is considering whether to hold a press conference about the mandamus application in which he elaborates on and defends his ruling. Which of the following statements most accurately states his options under the Model Code of Judicial Conduct?

(A) The judge is free to hold the press conference regarding the mandamus proceeding because it is not pending in his court.

(B) The judge may hold the press conference because in the mandamus proceeding he is the respondent.

(C) The judge may not personally appear at the press conference but may have his clerk act as his spokesperson to comment on the mandamus proceeding.

(D) The judge may not hold the press conference if his statements might reasonably be expected to affect the outcome or impair the fairness of the mandamus proceeding.

128. Judge Rosalie Reed has just been assigned to a new case and has realized that her domestic partner's sister's husband will be a material witness in the proceeding. The judge is firmly convinced that, despite this coincidence, there is no basis upon which her impartiality could reasonably be questioned. Which of the following statements most accurately describes the judge's responsibilities under the Model Code of Judicial Conduct?

(A) The judge must recuse herself because the witness is too closely related to the judge's domestic partner's sister.

(B) The judge must recuse herself because the witness is related to the judge's domestic partner's sister.

(C)   The judge must not recuse herself because the relationship between the judge and the witness is too remote.

(D)   The judge must not recuse herself because the judge is firmly convinced that, despite the distant relationship to the witness, the judge's impartiality could not reasonably be questioned.

129.   Judge Omar Fayid has just been presented with an emergency application for temporary restraining order to prevent the foreclosure sale of an office building that is the only asset of a corporation in which his grandson owns a substantial interest. It is a holiday weekend, and no other judges of the court are or will be available to rule on the application before the foreclosure sale is scheduled. Which of the following statements most accurately reflects the judge's obligations under the Model Code of Judicial Conduct?

(A)   The judge must rule on the application, disclose the basis for his disqualification, and make reasonable efforts to transfer the case to another judge as soon as practicable.

(B)   The judge has the option to hear and rule on the application because no other judge is available.

(C)   The judge must recuse himself from ruling on the application because of his grandson's financial interest in the case.

(D)   The judge may hear and rule on the application because his grandson does not personally have a direct financial stake in the case.

130.   Judge Tomeika Jones is assigned to the domestic relations caseload for her court. Over the last several months, she has noticed that attorney Leo Duncan has been having increasing difficulty representing his clients at the afternoon docket calls. Leo is elderly. In the mornings, Leo is fine, but in the afternoon, he appears to be forgetful and agitated, although he does not seem to be intoxicated or otherwise under the influence. His condition, whatever it may be, is impairing his ability to represent his clients, although the judge does not believe it has yet risen to the level of a violation of the Rules of Professional Conduct. Which of the following statements most accurately describes the judge's options under the Model Code of Judicial Conduct?

(A)   The judge may take any appropriate action that is reasonably likely to address the problem and prevent harm to the justice system.

(B)   The judge must refer Leo to a lawyers assistance program.

(C)   The judge must take any appropriate action that is reasonably likely to address the problem and prevent harm to the justice system.

(D)   The judge must report Leo to the disciplinary authorities.

131.   Judge Devin Howell is a faithful member of the local "Endzone Club," a local civic organization devoted to economic development. He always attends the club's annual fall dinner. It is a tradition at these dinners for local community leaders to "roast" one of their own. At the most recent dinner, Judge Howell made a series of jokes about the

African-American mayor that could only be described as racist. The judge affected a dialect and joked about several traditional stereotypes of "Negroes." The audience cringed at these inappropriate attempts at humor. Which of the following statements most accurately describes the propriety of these remarks under the Model Code of Judicial Conduct?

(A) The judge did not violate the Code because the judge was joking.

(B) The judge did not violate the Code because the jokes were not made in a judicial capacity.

(C) The judge violated the code because his jokes would appear to a reasonable person to undermine his impartiality.

(D) The judge violated the code because he engaged in extrajudicial activities not devoted to the law.

132. Judge Cory Becker lives in a growing part of his county. A local bank has applied for a change in zoning to permit a branch to be built next to the judge's home, which is in an area that for now is entirely residential. Judge Becker wishes to appear before the zoning board to testify against the change. Which of the following statements most accurately reflects the judge's options under the Model Code of Judicial Conduct?

(A) The judge may not appear before the zoning board unless a party in interest subpoenas him to testify.

(B) The judge may appear before the zoning board because the subject matter of the hearing concerns the law.

(C) The judge may not appear before the zoning board because the judge would be misusing the prestige of his judicial office.

(D) The judge may appear before the zoning board because he is acting pro se.

133. Judge Gregory Hubbard was a member of the Southern Heritage Golf Club before his election to the bench. Judge Hubbard knew, and the disciplinary authorities in his state had previously found, that the club practiced invidious discrimination on the basis of race, sex, and religion. Before he took his oath of office, Judge Hubbard resigned from the club. Judge Hubbard's daughter was recently married and needed a place to hold the reception. To make sure his daughter had the best, Judge Hubbard rented the banquet hall of the Golf Club for his daughter's wedding reception. Which of the following statements most accurately describes the propriety of Judge Hubbard's actions under the Model Code of Judicial Conduct?

(A) Judge Hubbard violated the code because he used the facilities of an organization that practiced invidious discrimination on the basis of race, sex, and religion.

(B) Judge Hubbard violated the code because he attended an event at the facilities of an organization that practiced invidious discrimination on the basis of race, sex, and religion.

(C) Judge Hubbard did not violate the code because he resigned from the club before he became a judge.

    (D)   Judge Hubbard did not violate the code because his use of the club's facilities was an isolated event.

134. Judge Claudia Malone has been asked by her local Inn of Court (an organization devoted to the promotion of excellence, civility, and professionalism among members of the trial bar) to be in charge of soliciting members for the upcoming year. Members pay dues that are used to support the Inn. Which of the following statements most accurately describes Judge Malone's options under the Model Code of Judicial Conduct?

    (A)   The judge may solicit membership, but only from members of the judge's family and from judges over whom the judge does not have supervisory or appellate authority.

    (B)   The judge may solicit membership because the organization is concerned with the administration of justice.

    (C)   The judge may not solicit membership because doing so is inherently coercive.

    (D)   The judge may not solicit membership because membership requires the payment of money.

135. Judge Maxwell Blake has a son who attends college in another part of the state. Late one Friday night, Judge Blake receives a telephone call from which he learns that his son has been arrested for drug trafficking and is incarcerated at the county jail. His son's first appearance is to be at 8 a.m. Saturday in the courtroom at the jail. Which of the following most accurately describes Judge Blake's options under the Model Code of Judicial Conduct?

    (A)   The judge may represent his son in the criminal case.

    (B)   The judge may represent his son only at the first appearance because there is insufficient time to obtain other counsel.

    (C)   The judge may represent his son in the criminal case as long as the judge does not use the prestige of his judicial office to advance his son's interests.

    (D)   The judge may not represent his son at the first appearance or otherwise.

136. Judge Frank Stuart is a veteran of Operation Iraqi Freedom, and in fact is a decorated war hero. He has received an offer from a publishing company to pay him royalties if he will write, and allow the company to publish, his memoir of the war. Which of the following statements most accurately describes the judge's options under the Model Code of Judicial Conduct?

    (A)   The judge may accept the offer if the royalties are reasonable and commensurate with the task performed.

    (B)   The judge may accept the offer if writing the book would not appear to a reasonable person to undermine the judge's independence, integrity, or impartiality.

    (C)   The judge may not accept the offer because writing a book about something other than the law is not a permitted extrajudicial activity.

(D) The judge may not accept the offer if writing the book would interfere with the performance of his judicial duties.

137. Judge Erma Boyd is in the process of buying a house. One of the local banks has offered the judge a mortgage, at a rate that is one-quarter of one-percent below their usual rate. The bank officer explained the difference by stating that the bank "made a business judgment that it is less risky to loan money to a judge than it is to loan to other people." Under the Model Code of Judicial Conduct, may the judge accept the discounted rate on her mortgage?

(A) The judge may accept the discount only if the bank is not a party to a case in her court.

(B) The judge may accept the discount only if the bank is not currently or frequently a party in her court.

(C) The judge may not accept the discount because it is not available to people who are not judges.

(D) The judge may not accept the discount because judges are not permitted to accept commercial discounts.

138. Judge Mason Evans has been invited to a seminar about drug litigation in Cancun. The seminar is being put on by a trade association, Better Living Through Pharmaceuticals (BLTP). BLTP is funded by major drug companies. The judge presides over a docket that includes a fair number of product liability cases involving drugs. Judge Evans has been invited to speak at the seminar and attend the sessions free of charge, and BLTP has offered to pay his expenses. Which of the following statements most accurately reflects the judge's options under the Model Code of Judicial Conduct?

(A) Judge Evans may not accept reimbursement of his expenses under these circumstances.

(B) Judge Evans may accept the reimbursement as long as he receives only the actual costs reasonably incurred by the judge.

(C) Judge Evans may accept reimbursement of the expenses as long as he publicly reports them.

(D) Judge Evans may accept the reimbursement of his expenses as long as they are associated with the judge's participation in extrajudicial activities permitted by the Code.

139. Judge Amanda Reeves is a widow but has maintained a close familial relationship with her deceased husband's elderly parents. They have asked the judge to serve as trustee for irrevocable trusts that they wish to establish for the management of their financial affairs as they age. The judge's service as trustee would take very little time, and she has no reason to believe that the trusts or its beneficiaries would ever be litigants in her court. She also has no reason to believe that her service as trustee will require her ever to disqualify herself from cases on her docket or otherwise interfere with the proper performance of her judicial duties. Which of the following statements most accurately describes the propriety of the judge's service as trustee under the Model Code of Judicial Conduct?

(A)   The judge may act as trustee because judges may act as fiduciaries as long as doing so will not interfere with the proper performance of their judicial duties.

(B)   The judge may act as trustee because her deceased husband's parents are members of the judge's family.

(C)   The judge may not act as trustee because she is not related to her deceased husband's parents.

(D)   The judge may not act as trustee because judges are not permitted to serve in this capacity.

140.   Judge Clayton Saunders is presiding over a civil case in which a pro se plaintiff is suing a corporate defendant that is well represented. The plaintiff is unfamiliar with the law and with court procedure, and as a result is in danger of having his case dismissed without it being heard on the merits. Which of the following statements most accurately reflects the judge's options under the Model Code of Judicial Conduct?

(A)   The judge must enforce court procedures as to a pro se party just as the court would enforce them against an attorney representing a party.

(B)   The judge must appoint counsel to ensure that the pro se litigant has the opportunity to have the matter fairly heard.

(C)   The judge may make reasonable accommodations to ensure that the pro se litigant has the opportunity to have the matter fairly heard.

(D)   The judge must make reasonable accommodations to ensure that the pro se litigant has the opportunity to have the matter fairly heard.

141.   Judge Johanna Mills learns from a presentencing report that a convicted felon whom she will be sentencing has said that his fellow gang members "will take care of" and "cap" the court deputy who was assigned to guard the defendant during trial. Judge Mills wishes to warn the deputy about this threat. Which of the following statements most accurately describes the judge's options under the Model Code of Judicial Conduct?

(A)   The judge may warn the deputy because the judge may use nonpublic information to protect court personnel.

(B)   The judge may warn the deputy because the judge is permitted to reveal and use information that the judge learns in her official capacity.

(C)   The judge may not warn the deputy because the information in the presentencing report is nonpublic information.

(D)   The judge may not warn the deputy because the presentencing report is confidential.

142.   Judge Val Silva is presiding over a hotly-contested case involving the dissolution of a closely-held business. The judge has just received and read a letter that was faxed to his

office. It appears that the letter, which was written by plaintiff's counsel and is addressed to the plaintiff, was faxed by mistake to the judge. Which of the following statements most accurately describes the judge's responsibilities under the Model Code of Judicial Conduct?

(A) The judge must notify the sender that the judge inadvertently received the letter.

(B) The judge must return the communication to the plaintiff's counsel and notify all parties that he has done so.

(C) The judge must notify all parties of the substance of the communication and provide them with an opportunity to respond.

(D) The judge must destroy the document because it was inadvertently sent.

143. Judge Jayson Laird began his career as a police officer. One of his most memorable cases involved a heinous violent crime perpetrated by Skip Johnson. Judge Laird has just learned that Skip Johnson is a defendant to several felony charges that are to be heard in Judge Laird's court. Laird knows so much about Johnson's past that, if he is honest with himself, he would have to say that the very thought of Johnson sickens him. For some reason, neither Johnson nor Johnson's lawyer seem to be aware of the judge's past experience with Johnson, and no one has made a motion to disqualify the judge. Which of the following statements most accurately reflects Judge Laird's responsibilities under the Model Code of Judicial Conduct?

(A) Judge Laird must recuse himself if a motion to disqualify is made.

(B) Judge Laird must disqualify himself.

(C) Judge Laird must disclose his prejudice on the record and disqualify himself unless all parties stipulate to his remaining on the case.

(D) Judge Laird may recuse himself because he has a personal prejudice concerning a party.

144. Judge Anita Hornsby has been asked by her state's governor to be a member of the Special Commission on Juvenile Court Reform. The judge wants to serve because she is a former Juvenile Court judge, although now she has no jurisdiction, appellate or otherwise, over juvenile matters. Which of the following statement most accurately describes the judge's options under the Model Code of Judicial Conduct?

(A) The judge may not accept the appointment.

(B) The judge may accept the appointment because it concerns the law.

(C) The judge may accept appointments to government commissions as long as they do not interfere with the proper performance of judicial duties.

(D) The judge may accept the appointment because she has particular expertise about the subjects the commission will be studying.

145. Judge Alan Cooper was recently appointed to the bench. The judge has for years been an usher as part of the Sunday morning service at First United Methodist Church. Every service includes a hymn during which collection plates are passed among the congregation. Which of the following statements most accurately reflects Judge Cooper's responsibilities under the Model Code of Judicial Conduct?

   (A) The judge may continue to attend the services and serve as an usher.

   (B) The judge may attend the entire service but may not serve as an usher because doing so undermines the prestige of his judicial office.

   (C) The judge may attend the entire service but may not serve as an usher because doing so is inherently coercive.

   (D) The judge may not attend any part of the service that serves a fund-raising purpose.

146. Judge Bert Riley is presiding over a case involving a fire that was allegedly caused by aluminum wiring in a house. The judge did not understand part of the testimony of one of the experts and, without thinking, took his smart phone from his pocket and googled the term "COPALUM crimp connector," which apparently was the technique used by the defendant to minimize the risk of fire. The judge wanted to learn more about what the defendant did. Before he read the results of the search, the judge paused to think about whether what he was doing was proper under the Model Code of Judicial Conduct. Which of the following statements most accurately reflects the judge's options under the Model Code of Judicial Conduct?

   (A) The judge must not view the results of his search.

   (B) The judge is free to view the results of his search if doing so would assist the judge in the discharge of his judicial responsibilities.

   (C) The judge may review the results of the search if he first informs counsel for both parties of his search and provides them with adequate opportunity to address the results of the judge's research.

   (D) The judge may review the results of the search if he later informs counsel for both parties of his search and provides them with adequate opportunity to address the results of the judge's research.

147. Judge Wade Harvey is presiding over a high-profile case involving the paternity and custody of a celebrity's baby. One of the parties has made statements to the media in which she alleges that the judge has committed judicial misconduct in the way he has handled the trial so far. Which of the following statements most accurately describes the judge's options under the Model Code of Judicial Conduct?

   (A) The judge may not respond to the allegations personally but may have a member of the court staff respond to them.

   (B) The judge may not respond publicly to the allegations until the conclusion of the trial.

(C)   The judge may respond to the allegations if the response is truthful and reasonably related to the facts that underlie the claim of misconduct.

(D)   The judge may respond publicly to these allegations as long as his response will not substantially interfere with the fairness of the trial.

148. In the midst of her heated recent reelection campaign, Judge Shirley Perkins made a speech in which she stated that the "civil union" statute recently passed by her state's legislature violates the state constitution's guarantee of equal protection of the laws and that she would so rule — unlike her opponent — if such a challenge reached her court. A suit challenging the constitutionality of this statute on this basis has been filed and is now pending in the judge's court. Under the Model Code of Judicial Conduct, which of the following statements most accurately describes the judge's options?

(A)   The judge may hear the case because her opinion about this issue was formed from an extrajudicial source, her own independent reading and study of the question.

(B)   The judge must recuse herself if her impartiality might reasonably be questioned.

(C)   The judge must recuse herself from the case.

(D)   The judge may hear the case if she is able to decide the case impartially and without regard to her campaign statement.

149. Joel Meyer is an attorney who belongs to an independent conservative Christian church that does not permit gay or lesbian members, as a matter of religious belief and interpretation of the Bible. Mr. Meyer is considering a campaign to become a trial court judge but is concerned that his membership in his church would put him in violation of the rules of conduct for judges. Which of the following statements most accurately describes how the Model Code of Judicial Conduct would apply to Mr. Meyer's concern?

(A)   As a judge, Mr. Meyer would have to resign immediately from any organization that practiced invidious discrimination based upon sexual orientation.

(B)   Mr. Meyer could serve as judge without concern because the Model Code of Judicial Conduct does not prohibit membership in organizations that practice invidious discrimination based upon sexual orientation.

(C)   Mr. Meyer could serve as a judge without resigning from his church because his membership in the church is a lawful exercise of his freedom of religion.

(D)   Mr. Meyer could serve as a judge only if he resigned from his church within a reasonable time after taking office.

150. Judge Hope McKinney is a proud alumna of Centerville High School. In honor of the school's 50th anniversary, the headmaster wants to send out a letter from the "Thank You Centerville Committee," a group of distinguished alums of the school. The letter would be a solicitation for contributions to the "Next Fifty Years Fund," an endowment to help the school continue to thrive. The draft letterhead that the Committee would use for this letter has just arrived, and it lists the judge as "The Honorable Hope McKinney, Judge of 111th

Superior Court, Class of '84" and also lists all of the other members of the Committee. The judge gives her permission for this use of her name and title. Which of the following statements most accurately describes the propriety of the judge's decision under the Model Code of Judicial Conduct?

(A) The judge's decision complies with the Code if the listings for other members of the Committee also contain comparable designations of their professional status.

(B) The judge's decision complies with the Code because the money is being solicited for educational purposes.

(C) The judge's decision violates the Code because it uses the prestige of her judicial office for non-judicial purposes.

(D) The judge's decision violates the Code because judges are not permitted to participate in fund-raising.

151. Judge Edward Owens is not sure, but he reasonably believes, that one of the attorneys in a case in his court has destroyed evidence that would have been discoverable by the other party. Under the Model Code of Judicial Conduct, what options, if any, does the judge have, now that he has formed this reasonable belief?

ANSWER:

152. Judge Frank Clarke recently rendered summary judgment in a zoning appeal regarding a proposed shopping center. His ruling caused the market value of a nearby parcel of undeveloped land to double overnight. Judge Clarke has just learned to his surprise that the undeveloped land is owned by Judge Clarke's church, which he serves as a member of the Board of Trustees. How, if at all, did Judge Clarke violate the Model Code of Judicial Conduct?

ANSWER:

153. Judge Leona Hughes is presiding over the grand jury, which has been investigating the real estate deals of one of the leading candidates for governor. The judge knows from the grand jury proceedings that the candidate is very likely guilty of some serious crimes and at the very least is a demonstrably corrupt man. To save the electorate from making the mistake of electing him governor, the judge leaks the grand jury testimony to a reporter. Has the judge violated the Model Code of Judicial Conduct, given that the judge did not have a self-interested motive?

ANSWER:

154. Conrad Keller is an attorney who is campaigning to be elected as a judge. He has received a questionnaire from the "Justice Delayed is Justice Denied Committee." The questionnaire asks for Conrad's commitment to starting court on time every day and streamlining the court administration to reduce the backlog of cases. How, if at all, may Conrad respond to the questionnaire?

ANSWER:

155. Judge Tommy Buchanan has just learned that his ex-wife will be the attorney for one of the parties to a contested divorce in his court. The judge bears no ill will toward his ex-wife. Under what circumstances, if any, must the judge recuse himself from this new case?

ANSWER:

156. Judge Holly Phelps has been invited to speak at and attend her state bar's annual meeting. The bar has offered to reimburse the judge for the costs of her travel, food, and lodging expenses and for the travel, food, and lodging expenses of her husband (who is not a lawyer). Under what circumstances, if any, may the judge accept reimbursement of expenses for herself and her husband?

ANSWER:

157. Graham Carruthers is an attorney running for a seat on his state's Supreme Court. Judicial races in his state are non-partisan. The state is lopsidedly Democratic, and Graham has been a faithful Democratic Party loyalist for decades and is the hand-picked candidate of the Democratic governor. Under the Model Code of Judicial Conduct, how, if at all, may Graham use the endorsement of the state Democratic Party in his race for the Supreme Court?

ANSWER:

158. Judge Andrea Bridges has just been told by one of the other judges on her court that he recently sentenced a repeat drug offender to a period of probation "because the kid's Dad and I go way back, and the Dad is one of my biggest campaign contributors." Under the Model Code of Judicial Conduct, what responsibility, if any, does Judge Bridges now have?

ANSWER:

159. Judge Ben Brown is an adjunct professor at the local law school. At the end of the academic year, the first-year class voted him "Teacher of the Year" and gave him a trophy to display in his chambers. Under the Model Code of Judicial Conduct, must Judge Brown reject or report this gift?

ANSWER:

160. Judge Cary Parsons is married to a woman whose primary occupation is as a sales associate to a real estate broker. Every year, the broker gives a prize to the sales associate in the office that generates the greatest volume of sales. This year, the prize was a 50-inch 3-D television, and it

went to the judge's wife. Under the Model Code of Judicial Conduct, what obligation, if any, does the judge have to insist on rejection of, or to report, the television?

ANSWER:

PRACTICE FINAL EXAM: QUESTIONS

PRACTICE FINAL EXAM

Suggested Completion Time: Two Hours.

There are 36 multiple-choice questions and 12 short-answer questions. Allow one hour for the multiple-choice section of the exam (about 90 seconds per question) and one hour for the short-answer section (five minutes per question).

161. Melinda Briggs is an attorney who is representing Biff McCloud in connection with Biff's divorce. In a telephone call, Biff tells Melinda "I am going to load my gun and go and kill that no good wife of mine." Melinda knows Biff well enough to know that Biff is just blowing off steam. She does not believe it is necessary to do anything to protect Biff's wife. Which of the following statements best describes Melinda's responsibilities under the Model Rules of Professional Conduct?

    (A) Melinda may warn Biff's wife about Biff's threat.

    (B) Melinda must warn Biff's wife about Biff's threat.

    (C) Melinda may not warn Biff's wife about Biff's threat.

    (D) Melinda must withdraw from representing Biff.

162. Calico Insurance Company believes that it can save money by hiring salaried "staff counsel" to represent its policyholders in litigation rather than referring those cases to outside counsel. Which of the following statements best describes the responsibilities of lawyers acting as staff counsel for an insurance company under the Model Rules of Professional Conduct?

    (A) Staff counsel may not represent Calico's policyholders because there is a conflict of interest between their employer, the insurance company, and the clients, the policyholders.

    (B) Staff counsel may represent policyholders as long as the lawyers practice in a law firm setting and practice under a law firm trade name.

    (C) Staff counsel may represent policyholders as long as the lawyers disclose their employment status and exercise independent professional judgment on behalf of the policyholders.

    (D) Staff counsel may represent policyholders only in matters that would be fully covered by the insurance policy because otherwise there would be a conflict of interest between their employer, the insurance company, and the clients.

163. Sam Guzman is in-house counsel for IBOT, Inc., a leading manufacturer of household robots. The CEO of IBOT assigns Sam to investigate some allegations that IBOT exported sensitive nanotechnology to Iran, in violation of U.S. export laws. Any such violation would

67

cause IBOT to incur steep fines and other sanctions. Sam investigates and discovers illegal exports have occurred but that the State Department is running an "amnesty program" under which IBOT would escape the much more serious punishment that will otherwise follow. Despite taking this information and his recommendation all the way to the Board of Directors, IBOT declines to tell the State Department about what it has done. Sam tells the State Department himself and is promptly fired. Which of the following statements best describes the propriety of Sam's disclosure under the Model Rules of Professional Conduct?

(A) Sam had the option to disclose because his client had violated the law.

(B) Sam had the option to disclose because he had taken the matter to the Board of Directors without success and he acted to protect his client.

(C) Sam was required to reveal that his client had violated the law.

(D) Sam did not have the option to reveal because he learned the information in the course of investigating the matter.

164. Cindy Perez is an attorney who represents an individual in litigation against Ginormous, Inc., which is represented by a large local law firm. One day, Cindy receives a telephone call about the case from Dash Stone, an in-house attorney working for Ginormous. Which of the following statements best describes Cindy's responsibilities under the Model Rules of Professional Conduct?

(A) Cindy may speak with Dash because Dash is an in-house attorney for Ginormous, even though he is not counsel of record in the case.

(B) Cindy may not speak with Dash because Ginormous is represented by counsel.

(C) Cindy may speak with Dash as long as she obtains the consent of outside counsel for Ginormous.

(D) Cindy may speak with Dash even though Ginormous is represented by counsel because Dash initiated the contact.

165. Herman Schmidt is an attorney who is easily recognized in his small town because of his shaved head. He has decided to take advantage of that recognition by marketing his practice under the trade name, "The Bald Lawyer Law Offices." Which of the following statements best describes the propriety of Herman's plan under the Model Rules of Professional Conduct?

(A) Herman may not practice using a trade name.

(B) Herman may practice using this trade name.

(C) Herman may not practice using this trade name because it is undignified.

(D) The Model Rules of Professional Conduct do not address the propriety of trade names.

166. Julie Fuller is an attorney who has encountered a problem for a client that she has never seen before. She would like to consult one of her former law professors about the problem. Which of the following statements best describes her options under the Model Rules of Professional Conduct?

(A) Julie may not discuss the case with her former professor because she would be violating her duty of confidentiality.

(B) Julie may discuss the case with her former professor as long as she discusses it as a hypothetical and there is no reasonable likelihood that the professor could identify the client or the matter.

(C) Julie may discuss the case with her former professor because such disclosure is impliedly authorized as part of the representation.

(D) Julie may discuss the case with her former professor as long as the professor commits to keeping the matter confidential.

167. Allan Murray and Mitchell Banks are partners in the firm of Murray & Banks. Allan is the "office" lawyer and Mitchell is the "courthouse" lawyer. Last year, Allan represented Don Huddleston in the creation of Don's estate plan. Allan created a trust, drafted a will, and prepared the other documents that Don needed to effect his plan for his estate. In conformity with firm policy, Allan sent Don a letter when the work was done to notify Don that Allan was no longer his lawyer but would welcome the opportunity to discuss future representation. Allan has since heard that Don fell on hard times and filed bankruptcy. Mitchell has now been asked by a new client to represent that client against Don and allege that Don committed bankruptcy fraud when he filed a deliberately incomplete list of his assets with the bankruptcy court. Under the Model Rules of Professional Conduct, which of the following most accurately describes the proper response to the new client's request under the Model Rules of Professional Conduct?

(A) The firm may not represent the new client without Don's consent to the conflict of interest.

(B) Mitchell may represent the new client as long as Allan is screened from any participation in the fraud case.

(C) The firm may represent the new client because the two matters are not substantially related.

(D) The firm may represent the new client with the informed consent of the new client to the conflict of interest.

168. Saul Greenberg is a young associate at Finster & Smith, a large urban law firm. Saul recently completed his clerkship with United States District Judge Jerry McMillan. Part of Saul's work for Judge McMillan consisted of an extensive analysis of volumes of evidence and briefs related to a motion for summary judgment in the antitrust case of Mr. Waste, Inc. v. Waste Control, Inc. Saul did the first draft of the order that denied that motion. Now Finster & Smith has been asked to substitute as counsel in that case for Mr. Waste, Inc. Which of the following most accurately describes the propriety of the firm doing so under the Model Rules of Professional Conduct?

(A) The firm may substitute as counsel.

(B) The firm may not substitute as counsel without the informed consent of Mr. Waste, Inc. and Waste Control, Inc.

(C) The firm may substitute as counsel as long as Saul is screened from any participation in the matter, receives no part of the fee, and notice is given to all parties.

(D) The firm may not under any circumstances substitute as counsel.

169. Kerry O'Brien is an experienced attorney who specializes in child custody disputes. Several times in recent years, he has had to decline representation of one parent because the other parent had consulted him but chose not to hire him. He wishes to avoid or minimize that possibility in the future. Which of the following statements most accurately reflects Kerry's options under the Model Rules of Professional Conduct?

(A) He may represent the second parent as long as he took reasonable measures to avoid exposure to more qualifying information than was reasonably necessary to determine whether to represent the first parent.

(B) He may represent the second parent only if he took reasonable precautions to avoid learning any significantly harmful information and he learned no significantly harmful information from the first parent.

(C) He may represent the second parent only if the prospective client communicated significantly harmful information unilaterally, without any reasonable expectation that he was willing to discuss a lawyer-client relationship.

(D) With informed consent of the first parent, he may condition conversations with the first parent on an agreement that no information disclosed during the consultation will prohibit him from representing a different client in the matter and that he may use any such information subsequently.

170. Nathan Brewer is an attorney who represents plaintiffs in personal injury cases. He has had several cases recently that settled for less money than was appropriate just because the client needed money to pay bills and meet living expenses. Nathan wants to institute a new policy for his clients to try to ensure that they are financially able to wait for settlements that are fair. Which of the following statements most accurately describes Nathan's options under the Model Rules of Professional Conduct?

(A) Nathan may subsidize the reasonable living expenses of her clients as long as he does not expect to be repaid.

(B) Nathan may loan the client money for reasonable living expenses and make repayment contingent upon recovery in the case.

(C) Nathan may assist the client in obtaining a loan for reasonable living expenses and may personally guarantee that loan.

(D) Nathan may not provide financial assistance to a client for living expenses.

171. Cindy Barnett is a criminal defense attorney who has been asked to represent Viola Valdez, a former child movie star who has been accused of aggravated assault on her parents. Viola has no money from which she will be able to pay Cindy's fee. Which of the following statements most accurately describes Cindy's options under the Model Rules of Professional Conduct?

(A) Cindy may agree to take the case in exchange for literary rights to the story of Viola's arrest and trial.

(B) Cindy may not take the case on a contingent fee or in exchange for literary rights to the story of Viola's arrest and trial.

(C) Cindy may take the case on a contingent fee, on the assumption that Viola can raise the money for the fee by the sale of literary rights to the story of her arrest and trial after the trial is over.

(D) Cindy may permit Viola's agent to pay her fee anonymously.

172. Jack Bailey is an attorney whose practice consists entirely of business litigation. Jack recently negotiated a settlement of a large case, contingent upon approval of the settlement by the Board of Directors of Jack's client. A condition of the settlement going forward was that the opposing party gave Jack a check for $500,000, to be paid to Jack's client only upon approval of the settlement by the Board of Directors and execution of the appropriate releases. Several weeks later, Jack received an e-mail message from opposing counsel withdrawing the settlement offer based upon an allegation of fraud in the negotiations and demanding immediate return of the $500,000. Simultaneously, Jack received the signed releases and Board of Directors approval of the settlement from his client, along with a demand to pay to the client the $500,000. Which of the following statements most accurately describes Jack's options under the Model Rules of Professional Conduct?

(A) Jack must hold the $500,000 in his trust account until the dispute is resolved.

(B) Jack must return the $500,000 to the opposing party.

(C) Jack must pay the $500,000 to his client.

(D) Jack must decide who is entitled to the funds and pay the $500,000 to that party.

173. Delia Howard is a criminal defense attorney. Delia is defending "Spike" Washburn on charges of aggravated assault outside a nightclub. This would be Spike's third conviction for a violent felony. Spike tells Delia that he was asleep at his mother's house at the time of the crime. Numerous eyewitnesses have identified Spike as the assailant, and Spike has a distinctive appearance. Spike's mother refuses to corroborate Spike's alibi. Delia strongly suspects but of course does not know for sure that Spike is lying. Spike insists on testifying, which would enable the prosecution to use his prior convictions against him. Which of the following most accurately describes Delia's options under the Model Rules of Professional Conduct?

(A) Delia may refuse to let Spike testify.

(B)   Delia may allow Spike to testify but only by narrative rather than through questions from Delia.

(C)   Delia must allow Spike to testify.

(D)   Delia must seek to withdraw from representing Spike.

174.   Beau Granger is an attorney who recently completed the trial of a serious personal injury case. Beau represented the defendant, and part of the plaintiff's evidence was a heartbreaking "day in the life" video that depicted how the plaintiff's injuries affected her abilities to function on a day-to-day basis. The jury returned a large verdict for the plaintiff, and Beau's client decided to pay the judgment rather than appeal. The time for appeal has run. Beau has now learned that the "day in the life" video was a fraud. Beau knows that the plaintiff in fact suffered no injuries that affected her day-to-day life in the ways depicted in the video. Which of the following statements most accurately reflects Beau's options under the Model Rules of Professional Conduct?

(A)   Beau must take reasonable remedial measures with the tribunal to rectify the fraud.

(B)   Beau need not take reasonable remedial measures with the tribunal to rectify the fraud because the fraud has already occurred.

(C)   Beau can only take reasonable remedial measures with the tribunal to rectify the fraud after he obtains informed consent from his client to reveal the fraud because what Beau has learned is information relating to the representation.

(D)   Beau need not take reasonable remedial measures with the tribunal to rectify the fraud because the proceeding has concluded.

175.   Emery Sheldon is an attorney representing a client in civil litigation. Emery has in his possession a document that Emery firmly believes is covered by the client's privilege against self-incrimination. Emery's case is subject to a rule of court that requires privileged documents to be identified in discovery with particularity. Emery believes the rule is invalid in its application to his client's constitutional privilege. Which of the following statements most accurately describes Emery's options under the Model Rules of Professional Conduct?

(A)   Emery must obey the obligation imposed by the rule of the tribunal.

(B)   Emery may disobey the obligation because a constitutional right is involved.

(C)   Emery may disobey the obligation imposed by the rule of the tribunal as long as he does so openly based on an assertion that no valid obligation exists.

(D)   Emery must seek to withdraw from the representation because there is a significant risk that the representation will be materially limited by Emery's personal interest in obeying a rule of the tribunal.

176.   Lamar Bates is an attorney who has been asked to file a civil suit that will allege that the local university discriminates in its admissions policies against white students. Lamar is

unable to determine at this point whether there is an internal policy that results in a remarkably consistent percentage of minority students in the university, and he is aware that there is a precedent that is just five years old from the controlling court that holds that universities may take race into account in admissions. Which of the following statements most accurately describes Lamar's obligations under the Model Rules of Professional Conduct?

(A) Lamar may file the case even though he will need to develop facts in discovery and argue for the reversal of existing law.

(B) Lamar may file the case because the Rules of Professional Conduct, unlike rules of procedure, do not address the lawyer's role as "gatekeeper."

(C) Lamar may not file the case because he does not have vital evidence regarding the university's admissions policies.

(D) Lamar may not file the case because it is not warranted by existing law.

177. Jasmine Payne is an attorney who represents an insurance company in a dispute about coverage. Jasmine has interviewed her client's local agent, and Jasmine was not happy about what the agent said had been represented to the policyholder about the effect of the insurance. Jasmine knows that the policyholder's lawyer can take the deposition of this agent, but Jasmine does not want the agent to speak with the opposing lawyer voluntarily. Under the Model Rules of Professional Conduct, which of the following statements best describes the propriety of Jasmine requesting the agent not to do so?

(A) Jasmine may not make the request because the agent is not an employee of her client.

(B) Jasmine may not make the request because she may not impede another party's access to evidence.

(C) Jasmine may make the request as long as the agent's interests will not be adversely affected by refraining from giving such information.

(D) Jasmine may make the request because the witness is an agent of her client.

178. Conrad Adkins is an attorney who specializes in divorce actions. In negotiations for a property settlement with the husband of a client in a divorce case, his client tells Conrad that the client's husband defrauded the bank when he bought his home (before the client knew him) because the husband told the bank that the down payment came from a gift from his parents, when the "gift" was really a loan. The client instructs Conrad to threaten to tell the bank about the fraud if the property settlement is not sufficiently favorable to the client. Which of the following most accurately describes Conrad's obligations under the Model Rules of Professional Conduct?

(A) Conrad cannot threaten to reveal the fraud to further his client's position in a civil matter.

(B) Whether Conrad can make the threat depends upon whether doing so constitutes the crime of extortion in his jurisdiction.

(C) Conrad can threaten to reveal the fraud to assist in the negotiations as long as he makes no untruthful statements in the course of doing so.

(D) Conrad must make the threat, as long as doing so is not a crime, because his client has instructed him to do so.

179. Maria Hill is an attorney who has been appointed by a court to act as a mediator in a landlord-tenant dispute. At the mediation, Maria holds individual caucuses with the landlord, who is represented by counsel, and the tenant, who is unrepresented. During the caucus with the tenant, the tenant asks Maria whether the landlord can evict him if he refuses to pay his rent until some repairs are made. Which of the following statements most accurately describes Maria's responsibilities under the Model Rules of Professional Conduct?

(A) Maria must give a truthful response to the question.

(B) Maria must inform the tenant that she does not represent him and explain the difference between her role as a mediator and the role of an attorney representing a client.

(C) Maria may answer his question but only if she gives the same legal assessment to the landlord in her caucus with the landlord and the landlord's attorney.

(D) Maria must tell the tenant only that he should seek the advice of counsel.

180. Oren Perdue is a prosecutor who is overseeing the prosecution of a high-profile murder case. Oren has just learned that the sheriff is planning to hold a news conference at which the sheriff (who is running for reelection) will announce that the crime lab has just completed testing in the victim's home and has found traces of blood that match the defendant's DNA. Which of the following statements most accurately describes Oren's duties under the Model Rules of Professional Conduct?

(A) Oren has no obligation with respect to statements made by the sheriff.

(B) Oren will be vicariously liable as a disciplinary matter for any statements the sheriff makes.

(C) Oren has no obligation because this is a statement that Oren himself would be permitted to make.

(D) Oren must exercise reasonable efforts to stop the sheriff from making this statement.

181. Trevor Malleck is an attorney who was recently admitted to the bar. Trevor has a nagging fear that he did something in the bar admission process — or rather failed to do something — that could still get him in trouble. Trevor had pled guilty to felony possession of narcotics when he was 18 and was sentenced to probation. Trevor revealed this to the bar authorities, but somehow the staff report on his application ended up saying that Trevor had been sentenced as a "first offender" and that therefore he was never actually adjudicated guilty. Under the Model Rules of Professional Conduct, does Trevor have anything to worry about?

(A) Yes, because a felony conviction disqualifies him for membership in the bar.

(B) Yes, because he failed to disclose the truth to correct a misapprehension he knew had arisen in connection with his application.

(C) No, because he answered the questions truthfully on his bar application.

(D) No, because he was not a lawyer when he failed to reveal the truth.

182. Stephen Dunn is an attorney who specializes in closing residential real estate transactions. He also provides title insurance out of the same office, and to clients his provision of title insurance is not distinct from his provision of legal services. Which of the following best describes his obligations under the Model Rules of Professional Conduct with respect to the title insurance?

(A) Stephen must divest himself of the title insurance business.

(B) Stephen may operate the title insurance business and need not abide by the Rules of Professional Conduct in connection with it because in that business he is not acting as a lawyer.

(C) Stephen must not operate the title insurance business out of the same office as his law practice.

(D) Stephen may operate the title insurance business but must abide by the Rules of Professional Conduct in connection with his title insurance business.

183. Brooke Powell is an attorney who specializes in estate planning. Brooke has an arrangement with another firm, one that specializes in litigation against nursing homes. Brooke refers clients who need litigation to that firm, and that firm refers clients who need estate planning to Brooke. Which of the following statements best describes the propriety of this arrangement under the Model Rules of Professional Conduct?

(A) The arrangement is permissible with the informed consent of the clients.

(B) The arrangement is permissible as long as the lawyers do not share fees.

(C) The arrangement is not permissible because lawyers may not enter into reciprocal referral arrangements.

(D) The arrangement is not permissible if it is exclusive.

184. Vick & Costello is a law firm with offices in two states. Ms. Vick and five of the lawyers practice in, and are licensed only in, one state. Ms. Costello and the other three lawyers practice in, and are licensed only in, the other state. Under the Model Rules of Professional Conduct, which of the following statements most accurately describes the firm's options with respect to its letterhead?

(A) The firm may use the same name in both jurisdictions and may list each attorney by name on its letterhead but must indicate the jurisdictional limits on the rights of each attorney to practice.

(B)　The firm may not use the same name in both jurisdictions because neither of the named partners is licensed in both jurisdictions.

(C)　The firm may use the same name in both jurisdictions but must use letterhead for each office that lists only those attorneys licensed in that jurisdiction.

(D)　The firm may use the same name in each jurisdiction and may list each attorney by name on its letterhead.

185.　Ronald Maynard is an attorney in search of a plaintiff to challenge a new state health care law that requires uninsured individuals to purchase health insurance. Ronald is a retired lawyer and will be handling the case for free, simply because he believes in the autonomy of the individual. Ronald has asked Leslie Gordon to be the named plaintiff in this case. Leslie declined because Leslie does not want the notoriety and has made it clear that she does not want Ronald to solicit her again. Undeterred, Ronald is planning to ask her again if he can be her lawyer in a suit to invalidate the health care law. Under the Model Rules of Professional Conduct, which of the following statements most accurately describes the propriety of Ronald's plan?

(A)　Ronald's plan is permissible because he is not motivated even in part by pecuniary gain.

(B)　Ronald's plan is permissible as long as it does not involve coercion, duress, or harassment.

(C)　Ronald's plan is not permissible because Leslie has made known her desire not to be solicited by him.

(D)　Ronald's plan is not permissible because Ronald would be soliciting a prospective client.

186.　Rodney "The Jackhammer" Lockwood is an attorney who is planning an extensive advertising campaign to attempt to attract more business to his practice. He is eager to comply with the Model Rules of Professional Conduct, but he is willing to do anything within the rules. Which of the following marketing ideas is most likely to be found to be a violation of the Model Rules of Professional Conduct?

(A)　His statement of flat-rate fees for which he will do particular types of work.

(B)　His truthful descriptions of judgments he has obtained for other clients.

(C)　His tasteless and undignified "jackhammer" logo.

(D)　The areas of law to which he has limited his practice.

187.　Lucy Gaddis is a prosecutor who is supervising an undercover investigation into organized crime. She has been asked to authorize an informant to contact the target of the investigation directly. The target is known to be represented by counsel in connection with the activities that are suspected of being criminal. Under the Model Rules of Professional Conduct, which of the following statements most accurately reflects the propriety of the attorney authorizing the contact?

(A) The attorney may authorize the contact as long as it does not violate a constitutional right of the target.

(B) The attorney may authorize the contact because the lawyer is not making the contact himself.

(C) The attorney may not authorize the contact because the target is represented by counsel in the matter.

(D) The attorney may authorize the contact if it is deemed to be authorized by law because it is an undercover criminal investigation.

188. Pauline Weatherford is an attorney who represents Truax Enterprises, Inc. (TEI). TEI has been recruiting to fill an executive position in its branch office in Rio de Janeiro. The person selected is Liam Walters. Pauline wants to get Liam's employment agreement finalized. Liam does not have a lawyer and has not worked for an American company before. Pauline sends Liam a proposed contract, and it contains a covenant not to compete. Liam calls Pauline and asks her what that provision means. Under the Model Rules of Professional Conduct, which of the following correctly states Pauline's options in responding to this question?

(A) Pauline may advise Liam about the legal meaning of the covenant.

(B) Pauline cannot respond other than to suggest that Liam get a lawyer.

(C) Pauline may explain the term as long as she has explained that she represents an adverse party and not him.

(D) Pauline may secure the services of another lawyer in her firm to give Liam independent advice.

189. Judith Newsome is a senior associate at a large law firm. Her responsibilities include the direct supervision of a number of employees of the firm, including associates who do document review in the firm's largest case. She learned last week that one of these associates did not make a reasonably diligent effort to locate certain electronic documents that are responsive to a proper request from the opposing counsel. Judith nevertheless allowed the associate to serve the response to the request along with the few documents that were located, despite the insufficient search. Under the Model Rules of Professional Conduct, which of the following statements most accurately describes Judith's responsibility for the other attorney's lack of diligence?

(A) Judith is not responsible because she is not a partner in the firm.

(B) Judith is not responsible because she did not order the misconduct.

(C) Judith is responsible because the lawyer who committed the misconduct was under her supervision.

(D) Judith is responsible because she failed to take reasonable remedial action.

190. Carl Bannon is an attorney who wants to offer his clients a "one-stop shop" for legal services and accounting services. He has identified a local accounting firm, owned and operated by nonlawyers, with whom he would like to associate in some way. Under the Model Rules of Professional Conduct, which of the following statements most accurately describes his options?

    (A) Carl may arrange to offer accounting services by having the accounting firm become a wholly-owned subsidiary of his law firm.

    (B) Carl may allow his law firm to become a subsidiary of the accounting firm.

    (C) Carl may not associate in any way with the accounting firm.

    (D) Carl may form a partnership with the accounting firm and conduct a multi-disciplinary practice.

191. Harold Cooke represents a defendant and recently sent his paralegal to interview the victim whom his client injured. Harold knew the victim had retained counsel. Harold wanted to obtain a witness statement without interference from the victim's lawyer, and Harold's paralegal was able to accomplish this purpose, even though the paralegal made full disclosure about who she was and what she wanted. Under the Model Rules of Professional Conduct, which of the following statements most accurately reflects the propriety of Harold's actions?

    (A) Harold did not commit misconduct because the paralegal made the direct contact with the victim.

    (B) Harold did not commit misconduct because the paralegal's conduct did not involve dishonesty, fraud, deceit, or misrepresentation.

    (C) Harold committed misconduct by having his paralegal contact another lawyer's client directly on Harold's behalf.

    (D) Harold committed misconduct because a lawyer may contact an adverse party only through the formal processes of discovery.

192. Judge Scott Collins is a long-time member of the Cougars Club, a not-for-profit civic organization devoted to community service and the support of local charities. The judge is in line to be the next president of the Club, which would require him (under the by-laws of the Club) to be in charge of planning all the Club's fund-raising activities and of management of the Club's bank accounts and other investments. Under the Model Code of Judicial Conduct, which of the following statements most accurately describes the propriety of the judge serving in this capacity?

    (A) The judge may serve as president because the Cougars Club is a not-for-profit civic organization.

    (B) The judge may serve as president because doing so is an extrajudicial activity.

    (C) The judge may not serve as president because he would be planning fund-raising activities.

(D) The judge may not serve as president because he would be managing the Cougars Club's bank accounts and other assets.

193. Judge Howard Flores is a life-long baseball fan. He was thrilled to be asked to serve as a salary arbitrator under the terms of the Major League baseball collective bargaining agreement. The judge would hear evidence about the market value of players eligible for arbitration and choose either the salary requested by the player or the salary offered by the team. The judge would not charge for either his time or his expenses. The law of his jurisdiction neither expressly permits nor expressly prohibits judges from serving in such a capacity. Under the Model Code of Judicial Conduct, which of the following statements most accurately describes the propriety of the judge's participation?

(A) The judge may serve as a private arbitrator because doing so is not prohibited by the law of his jurisdiction.

(B) The judge may serve as a private arbitrator because he is doing so on a pro bono basis.

(C) The judge may not serve as a private arbitrator because acting as an arbitrator is a judicial function.

(D) The judge may not serve as a private arbitrator because doing so is not expressly authorized by the law of his jurisdiction.

194. Judge Sheila York is presiding over a criminal case when she realizes that many years ago she found the defendant guilty of an unrelated crime and sentenced him to prison. The judge remembers the case well and candidly has to admit to herself that she has a very low opinion of the defendant. The judge is unsure whether she must disqualify herself from the pending case because of a personal prejudice concerning a party because, after all, her feelings derive from an intra-judicial source rather than an extra-judicial source. The judge plans to call a law professor who specializes in judicial ethics and ask him whether she must disqualify herself. Under the Model Code of Judicial Conduct, which of the following statements most accurately describes the propriety of the judge's conduct?

(A) The judge may call the professor if she provides all parties with the opportunity to respond to any advice that the professor gives.

(B) The judge may call the professor because the purpose of her consultation is to determine whether her continued involvement in the pending case would be in compliance with the Code of Judicial Conduct.

(C) The judge may not call the professor unless she provides advance written notice of her intention to do so to all parties.

(D) The judge may not call the professor without the simultaneous participation of counsel for all parties because the conversation otherwise would be an ex parte communication.

195. Judge Emily Morgan is presiding over a murder trial in which a celebrity is accused of killing her live-in boyfriend. The judge has agreed to give interviews to a local magazine under the agreement that the interviews will not be published until after the case is over and all appeals have been exhausted. Because of this agreement, the judge has been

extraordinarily candid with the reporter, and has even stated that she believes that the defendant is "clearly guilty" and was "lying on the witness stand." Under the Model Code of Judicial Conduct, which of the following statements most accurately describes the propriety of the judge's comments?

(A) The judge's comments were proper because they were not public.

(B) The judge's comments were improper because they reflect a personal bias concerning a party to the proceeding.

(C) The judge's comments were improper because they might substantially interfere with a fair trial or hearing.

(D) The judge's comments were proper because they were not based on an extrajudicial source but instead were based entirely upon the evidence presented in open court.

196. Judge Norma Brownwell presides over major felony cases, and over 80% of the defendants in her court are indigent. Counsel for these indigent defendants is provided by court appointment of lawyers admitted to her court, on a rotating basis alphabetically. Judge Brownwell has just learned that the lawyer who made the highest financial contribution to her reelection campaign — the maximum allowed by law — has come up in the rotation and will be assigned the next case. Assigned lawyers are paid below-market rates for handling criminal cases. Which of the following statements most accurately describes Judge Brownwell's options under the Model Code of Judicial Conduct?

(A) The judge may appoint her contributor to the case because his name came up in the regular rotation.

(B) The judge may appoint her contributor to the case because the compensation is below-market.

(C) The judge may not appoint her contributor to the case because he was her primary contributor for her campaign.

(D) The judge may not appoint her contributor to the case because the lawyer will receive compensation for his work.

197. Sarah Price is an attorney who has been hired by Red Umbrella Insurance Company to defend one of its insureds, Jane Morden, in a personal injury action. The Insurance Company has just sent Sarah a lengthy memorandum about its "litigation procedures." The memo purports to limit the number of depositions that Sarah can take and places a very low ceiling on the amount of time she may bill for research. Sarah believes these limits are too severe for her to represent Jane competently. What are Sarah's options under the Model Rules of Professional Conduct?

ANSWER:

198. Carter Logan is an attorney who is representing an accountant in connection with a dispute between his client and the client's former business partners. Carter undertook the representation

on a contingent fee but has decided that was unwise because a substantial recovery for his client is unlikely. Trial is imminent. Carter wishes to renegotiate the fee arrangement to require his client to compensate him on an hourly basis for past and future work on the case. Under the Model Rules of Professional Conduct, is this change to the fee arrangement permissible?

ANSWER:

199. Finnegan & Gillespie is a large corporate law firm. Its standard engagement letter provides that clients will reimburse the firm for the disbursements that the firm makes in connection with the client's work. Because it is so large, the firm has arranged a special discount on its travel with one of the major airlines. Lawyers for the firm typically fly for 10% less than the standard coach rate that otherwise would be applicable. The executive committee of the firm is considering a policy under which the firm would charge clients the coach rate for travel and retain the 10% discount for itself, on the theory that the firm should be allowed to profit from the favorable arrangement it has been able to make with the airline. Under the Model Rules of Professional Conduct, under what circumstances, if any, may the firm adopt such a policy?

ANSWER:

200. Dirk Hickman was an in-house attorney with the United Daycare Corporation (UDD). Dirk learned that a particular vice president of UDD was making and enforcing rules that were endangering the safety of children at UDD's facilities, and Dirk knew that if any children were injured UDD would be held liable. Dirk took this information to his boss, the general counsel, who refused to do anything about it. Dirk then took the information to the Executive Vice President, and the general counsel promptly fired Dirk for insubordination. Dirk has now sued UDD for wrongful termination. Under the Model Rules of Professional Conduct, may Dirk reveal the information he learned about the danger to children at UDD facilities in order to establish his claim that he was fired for complying with his professional duties?

ANSWER:

201. Lillian Wood is an attorney who is representing a new client who has been arrested for possession of child pornography. The police acted on a tip and obtained a search warrant for the client's home, where they found computers and external hard drives loaded with hundreds of pornographic images. The client tells Lillian that the charges are all true. Lillian works with one secretary, two associates, and three paralegals. Under the Model Rules of Professional Conduct, does Lillian need informed consent from her client to reveal to her staff what she has learned from the client about thee charges?

ANSWER:

202. Wilhelmina Smith is an attorney who represents Andre Hamilton, an elderly plaintiff in a personal injury case. Wilhelmina has been negotiating with opposing counsel to settle the case. Just before appearing at a court status conference where Wilhelmina believes a final, favorable settlement can

be reached, Wilhelmina learns that her client has died. Must she reveal his death to the opposing party and/or the court?

ANSWER:

203. Lawrence Miller is an attorney who is representing a plaintiff in a personal injury case against a corporate defendant who is represented by a local law firm. The plaintiff was struck by a truck driven by an employee of the defendant. Lawrence has learned of the existence of three important witnesses. The first hired the driver of the truck and is now a former employee of the defendant. The second is a current, low-level employee of the defendant. This second person is a friend of the driver who had nothing to do with the accident but who may have had conversations with the driver. The third person is the driver, who is still employed by the defendant. None of these individuals have lawyers of their own. Lawrence would like to get their stories pinned down without the involvement of defense counsel. Under the Model Rules of Professional Conduct, may Lawrence contact one or more of these people without the consent of counsel for the defendant?

ANSWER:

204. Leon Davenport is an attorney who represents the plaintiff in a bitter lawsuit over a failed joint venture. Leon's client loathes the opposing party and that party's lawyer. Leon's client has instructed Leon to litigate this case as vigorously as Leon knows how and to make it as unpleasant as possible (within the rules of procedure) for the opposing party and the opposing lawyer. What are Leon's obligations under the Model Rules of Professional Conduct with respect to these instructions from the client?

ANSWER:

205. Clint Bailey has been appointed to represent Justin Little, who has been accused of involvement in a gang-related drug trafficking conspiracy. Justin is alleged to be a "retail" distributor at the street level. One of his co-defendants is Billy "Big Man" O'Malley, who is alleged to be one of the high-level "wholesale" members of the conspiracy. Clint formerly represented "Big Man" in connection with prior charges of the same nature, but Clint was able to have the charges dismissed after winning a suppression hearing. Under these circumstances, will the Model Rules of Professional Conduct allow Clint seek to avoid the appointment as counsel for Justin?

ANSWER:

206. Albert Cain is an attorney who has been asked to assist a neighbor by "ghostwriting" some pleadings that the neighbor will file in court pro se. Albert is concerned about the possibility that he will be found to have misled the court in which the pleadings are to be filed if he does not reveal that he wrote them or that he will be deemed to have engaged in some kind of dishonesty or deceit. Under the Model Rules of Professional Conduct, may Albert "ghostwrite" the pleadings without informing the court of his role?

ANSWER:

207. Damon Warner is an attorney whose brother Jacob is also an attorney. Damon currently practices law as a solo practitioner, and Jacob runs his own title insurance business. The two brothers want to form a partnership, Warner & Warner, and the new partnership would both practice law and sell title insurance. The brothers would be equal partners. Under the Model Rules of Professional Conduct, may the Warner brothers form their partnership?

ANSWER:

208. Darren Culbertson is a junior lawyer who is licensed in only one state. He has been asked by his boss to take several small depositions in a second state for the boss to use in a case pending in a third state. The boss is not licensed to practice law in the third state. Under what circumstances, if any, is Darren permitted to take the depositions in a state where he is not licensed?

ANSWER:

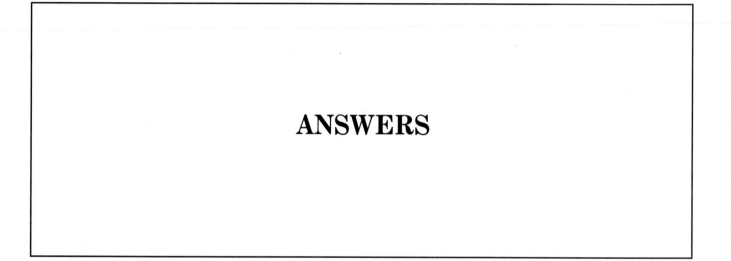

ANSWERS

1. **The correct answer is (A).** This is a disagreement between a lawyer and a client about the means of achieving the objectives of the representation (which presumably is to achieve the best result in the litigation). Rule 1.2(a) is quite clear that the lawyer "shall abide" by a client's decision about the objectives of the representation, but the lawyer's only stated obligation regarding means is that the lawyer "shall consult with the client." If the lawyer and the client cannot agree, then the impasse will be resolved either by the client firing the lawyer or the lawyer seeking to withdraw under Rule 1.16(b)(4) because of a fundamental disagreement. **Answers (B) and (D) are incorrect** because they purport to assign the right to decide about means to the lawyer and the client, respectively, whereas in fact Comment 2 to Rule 1.2 states that "this Rule does not prescribe how such disagreements are to be resolved." The resolution is expected ordinarily to emerge from the required consultation. **Answer (C) is incorrect** because the lawyer's duty to exercise independent professional judgment in giving advice does not dictate whose judgment prevails when the lawyer and the client disagree about the means to be employed in achieving the client's objectives. This answer implies that the lawyer has the authority to decide, even without consulting the client. The answer is wrong on both counts. Answer (A) is correct.

2. **The correct answer is (C).** This question involves the lawyer's duties of communication under Rule 1.4 and the duty to advise under Rule 2.1. The usual rule is that settlement offers in a civil case must be conveyed to the client because the client has a decision to make. See Rule 1.4(a)(1) (duty of communication when client's consent is needed) and Rule 1.2(a) (client has the right to decide whether to accept a settlement offer). Simply communicating the offer does not, however, discharge all of the attorney's responsibilities. **Answer (D) is incomplete and therefore incorrect.** However, there are some limited circumstances under which the lawyer need not tell the client about the offer, and if there is no need to convey the offer then obviously there is no need to render advice about it. Because there are such circumstances, **Answer (B)'s unequivocal requirement that the offer must be conveyed and the advice given is incorrect.** Comment 2 to Rule 1.4 makes it clear that a settlement offer need not be conveyed if the client has previously indicated that the offer would be unacceptable. **Answer (A) is incorrect** because, although it recognizes the possibility that the offer need not be conveyed to the client, it omits the requirement that the lawyer render her candid advice about the offer if it is conveyed. Answer (C), therefore, is correct. That answer includes the duties to communicate and advise, both qualified by the possibility that the client has already made it known to the lawyer that such an offer would be unacceptable.

3. **The correct answer is (C).** Because the court has not appointed the lawyer to the case, the lawyer is free to accept the client or not. The fee does not appear to be unreasonable under Rule 1.5(a), and therefore the lawyer has the choice simply to decline to represent someone who cannot pay that fee. The other answers are all incorrect. **Answer (A) is incorrect** because lawyers may not, under Rule 1.5(d)(2), charge contingent fees for representing a

defendant in a criminal case. **Answer (B) is incorrect** because Rule 1.8(e)·forbids lawyers from giving financial assistance, such as this loan to client, for living expenses. **Answer (D) is incorrect** because the lawyer has not been appointed to the case. If this had been a court appointment, the lawyer would have been under an obligation not to seek to avoid the appointment without good cause, such as an unreasonable financial burden. Because the court did not appoint the lawyer, he is free to accept the client or not. Therefore, Answer (C) is correct.

4.   **The correct answer is (D).** This hypothetical is based loosely upon the famous case of Alton Logan, who spent over 25 years in prison while two public defenders were silent about their knowledge that their client had committed the murder for which Mr. Logan was serving time. Under the current version of the Rules, the lawyer has the obligation, subject to certain exceptions, to keep confidential information relating to the representation. Rule 1.6. The scope of this confidentiality is much broader than the scope of the attorney-client privilege, and it would certainly encompass information learned from the relative in this case. **Answer (B), therefore, is incorrect.** The obligation of confidentiality is subject to some exceptions, however, so **Answer (C)'s categorical ban on disclosing the information is incorrect.** The relevant exception is found in Rule 1.6(b)(1), which provides that a lawyer may reveal confidential information if the lawyer reasonably believes doing so is necessary to prevent reasonably certain death or substantial bodily harm. This exception is optional, however, so **Answer (A) is incorrect.** Answer (D) correctly states the lawyer's option.

5.   **The correct answer is (C).** Absent consent, a lawyer cannot represent a client who is adverse in litigation to another of the lawyer's clients, even if the matters are unrelated. See Comment 6 to Rule 1.7. **Answer (A), therefore, is incorrect.** If one lawyer in the firm could not handle two matters because of Rule 1.7, two different lawyers may not do so, because the conflict is imputed under Rule 1.10(a) to all the lawyers in the firm. There is no exception to the general imputation rule for lawyers in the same firm who practice is different physical locations. **Answer (D), therefore, is incorrect. Answer (B) is incorrect** because it is possible (though unlikely) that the firm could obtain the informed consent of both clients to the two representations. There is nothing in the question to suggest that the lawyers in different offices of the firm would not be able each to provide competent and diligent representation to the clients. Therefore, the conflict would be consentable, and Answer (B) would be incorrect. Answer (C) is correct because it provides for the possibility of client consent.

6.   **The correct answer is (B).** Rule 1.8(j) prohibits an attorney from having a sexual relationship with a client unless the consensual sexual relationship existed at the time of the creation of the lawyer-client relationship. In this question, the lawyer and the client were not already in a sexual relationship. **Answer (D) is incorrect** because it supposes that the lawyer can have a sexual relationship with a client under these circumstances as long as she obtains informed consent. Rule 1.8(j) does not have an exception for consent. **Answer (C) is not the best answer,** because, although it correctly describes some of the concerns that underlie the prohibition on lawyer-client sexual relations, the rule is a categorical one. **Answer (A) is incorrect** because it permits the sexual relationship that the rule flatly proscribes. Answer (B) correctly states the choice that the lawyer faces: she must either refrain from commencing a sexual relationship or she must cease being the lawyer for this client.

7. **The correct answer is (A).** Alexander has a conflict of interest under Rule 1.9(b) if he joins L & M because he worked for clients in the Common Cases at his old firm. If L & M does nothing, that conflict will be imputed to all the lawyers in the firm under Rule 1.10(a). **Answer (C), therefore, is incorrect.** However, Rule 1.10(a)(2) allows the firm to escape from the imputation if it screens the incoming lawyer (and gives the proper notices and certifications). **Answer (B)'s unequivocal answer that L & M would have a conflict of interest if Alexander joined the firm is, therefore, incorrect.** Similarly, **Answer (D) is incorrect** because, although it states one circumstance under which Alexander could join the firm (consent of all affected clients), the answer incorrectly states that this is the only solution. Answer (A) is correct.

8. **The correct answer is (D).** George has a personal interest conflict. He presumably would find it difficult to litigate as vigorously for this client as he should if the opposing lawyer was his wife. So if George was a litigator and had been given this case, he would clearly have a conflict (and it might not be consentable). However, George is not a litigator, and the conflict is based on his personal interest in domestic tranquility. Because he is a young associate, it is unlikely that other lawyers in the firm would feel constrained in representing the new client vigorously out of fear of upsetting George or his wife. Therefore, this is a personal interest conflict that is not imputed within the firm, under Rule 1.10(a)(1). **Answer (A) is incorrect** because the conflict will not be imputed. **Answer (B) is incorrect** because George's conflict of interest would be imputed to the firm if it was something other than a personal interest conflict, whether he worked on the case or not. **Answer (C) is incorrect** because there is no need for a screen — the conflict will not be imputed — and in any event this is not one of the special cases for which screens are the solution. Answer (D) is correct.

9. **The correct answer is (B).** The lawyer has information relating to the representation, and the client has refused to consent to its disclosure. The lawyer wants to act to protect the corporation, so superficially it would appear that Rule 1.13(c) would enable him to reveal. However, the lawyer does not have the authority to reveal under 1.13(c), because the lawyer learned the information while he was conducting an investigation of the client's alleged violation of the law. Rule 1.13(d). Nor does the lawyer have authority under Rule 1.6(b) to reveal, because 1.6(b)(2) and (3) would authorize disclosure only if the lawyer's services had been used in connection with the fraud. Answer (B), therefore, is a complete statement of the constraints that prevent the lawyer from revealing the information. **Answer (A) is incorrect** because consent is a sufficient but not necessary condition for a lawyer to reveal confidential information. The answer is much too categorical. **Answer (C) is incorrect** because the lawyer learned of the information while conducting an investigation of the client's alleged violation of the law. **Answer (D) is incorrect** because the exceptions for confidentiality that relate to a client causing financial harm require that the lawyer's services have been used, and that is not the case here. See Rule 1.6(b)(2) and (3). Answer (B) is correct.

10. **The correct answer is (D).** Under Rule 1.16(a)(2), a lawyer is obligated to withdraw if "the lawyer's physical or mental condition materially impairs the lawyer's ability to represent the client." This mandatory withdrawal, however, is subject to Rule 1.16(c), which requires the lawyer to seek court permission before withdrawing. Because of the need for court permission, **Answer (A) is incorrect. Answer (B) is incorrect** because withdrawal is mandatory rather than optional under these conditions. **Answer (C) is incorrect** because there is no provision for client consent to representation that has been materially impaired

by a physical condition. Answer (D) is correct.

11. **The correct answer is (D).** A lawyer who has a client whose diminished capacity makes the client vulnerable may, but need not, take reasonably necessary protective action if the client cannot protect himself. **Answer (B) is wrong** because this situation has gone beyond merely a circumstance of diminished capacity. If the client was not in danger or could act for himself, then it would be enough for the lawyer to comply with Rule 1.14(a) and simply do his best to maintain a normal client-lawyer relationship with the client. Here, however, there is a danger and an inability to act for himself, and as a result the option to take protective action under Rule 1.14(b) exists. **Answer (C) is wrong** because taking protective action is an option rather than a mandate. **Answer (A) is incorrect** because the lawyer is impliedly authorized to make necessary disclosures if the lawyer takes protective action, even if the client directs otherwise. See Comment 8 to Rule 1.14. Answer (D) correctly states the lawyer's option.

12. **The correct answer is (D).** Dana was a prospective client, and she told Steve significantly harmful information about her case. Steve, therefore, is disqualified from representing the opposing party in Dana's case under Rule 1.18(c). Steve's firm, KM, is also disqualified, because Steve did not take reasonable measures to avoid being exposed to more information than he needed in order to decide whether or not to represent Dana. He asked an open-ended question, and that is not taking reasonable precautions. See Rule 1.18(d)(2). **Answer (A) is incorrect** because both Steve and KM are disqualified. **Answer (B) is incorrect** because screening is not available to KM to solve the problem. Screening would only have been available if the Steve had taken reasonable measures to avoid being exposed to too much information. **Answer (C) is incorrect** because Rule 1.18 requires disqualification of the lawyer and the firm under these circumstances and not just that they respect the prospective client's confidentiality. Furthermore, it is hard to imagine how Steve could represent Roger diligently under Rule 1.3 without at least using the significantly harmful information that he gathered from Dana. Answer (D) is the correct answer.

13. **The correct answer is (A).** Rule 1.15 governs the way in which lawyers must deal with funds in their trust accounts. Here, two people (one of whom is the lawyer) claim the same funds. Rule 1.15(e) requires in these circumstances that the lawyer keep the funds separate until the dispute is resolved. **Answer (B) is incorrect** because the lawyer cannot presume to decide this dispute unilaterally. **Answer (C) is incorrect** because the lawyer need not give up her claim until the dispute is resolved. See Comment 3 to Rule 1.15. **Answer (D) is incorrect** because interpleader is at most an option and not a mandate. See Comment 4 to Rule 1.5. Answer (A) is correct.

14. **The correct answer is (B).** First, it is important to recognize that any conflict that Clayton or his law partner have will be imputed to the other under Rule 1.10(a). **Answer (A) is therefore incorrect** because it does not matter that Clayton does not personally represent the roommate. **Answer (C) is incorrect** because this does not present one of the special cases in which screening can prevent the imputation of a conflict. See Rules 1.10(a)(2), 1.11(b), 1.12(c), and 1.18(d)(2) for examples of screening. **Answer (D) is incorrect** because this is not a consentable conflict. One lawyer could not provide competent and diligent representation to both Jimmy and the roommate, given that the roommate is helping himself by harming Jimmy. Therefore, under Rule 1.7(b)(1), this is not a conflict that can be solved by consent. There is no way to avoid the conflict. Answer (B) is therefore correct.

15. **The correct answer is Answer (C).** Although it is routine for lawyers to represent co-parties in civil litigation, the cross-claim would make the two clients adverse parties. Edward would, therefore, have a conflict of interest under Rule 1.7(a)(1) in asserting a claim for one client against another client. **Answer (B), therefore, is incorrect. Answer (A) is incorrect** because a conflict that arises in this way is a non-consentable conflict under Rule 1.7(b)(3). **Answer (D) is incorrect** because Edward's conflict would be imputed to all the lawyers associated with him in his firm under Rule 1.10(a). Answer (C) is correct.

16. **The correct answer is Answer (C).** Under Rule 1.9(a), the lawyer may not represent another person in the same (or a substantially related) matter if the new client's interests are materially adverse to the former client, unless the former client gives informed consent, confirmed in writing. Elsie is being asked to sue a former client, so her new client's interests are materially adverse to those of the former client. It is the same matter for which she represented BACC. Informed consent, confirmed in writing, is required, but, in the unlikely event that she can get such consent, she may file the suit. **Answer (A) is incorrect** because it is at least theoretically possible to sue her former client, with informed consent. **Answer (D) is incorrect** because consent from her former client is required, regardless of what the lawyer believes about her ability to act. **Answer (B) is incorrect** because, if Elsie is prohibited from representing John, then all the lawyers in her firm are also prohibited from doing so under Rule 1.10(a). This is not one of the limited situations in which screening the disqualified lawyer will solve the problem (compare Rules 1.11, 1.12, and 1.18), nor is the prohibition based upon a personal interest of the lawyer (compare Rule 1.8(j) and Comment 20 to Rule 1.8). Answer (C) is correct.

17. **The correct answer is (C).** TTS is a former client of the firm, and the firm has been asked to represent a new client is one of the same matters for which it represented TTS. That creates a conflict under Rule 1.9(a). There is a special rule for clients who leave the firm under circumstances like these. Under Rule 1.10(b), D & R could undertake representation of a new client against TTS, its former client, even in the same matter, if there were no lawyers remaining in the firm with confidential information about the matter. If that were true, then the primary harm that Rule 1.9 is supposed to prevent — the misuse of a former client's confidential information — would not be likely. Here, however, Oberlin is left behind, and therefore the special rule does not apply. **Answer (A) is incorrect** because this is not one of the special cases where screening solves a conflict of interest. **Answer (B) is tempting but is not the best answer.** It is true that the firm is switching sides, but it would be permitted to switch sides if there were no lawyers left in the firm with confidential information about the matter. It is Oberlin's continued association with the firm, rather than the fact that the firm is "switching sides," that creates the problem. **Answer (D) is incorrect** because firms are not allowed to undertake all new matters against a former client. In fact, the general rule is that the firm may not undertake new matters that are the same or are substantially related to matters that the firm handled for the former client. Answer (C) is correct because Oberlin's presence is what creates the conflict of interest.

18. **The correct answer is (A).** Rule 1.8(e) sets forth the limited circumstances under which an attorney can provide financial assistance to a client. One of those circumstances is that a lawyer may pay the expenses of litigation on behalf of an indigent client. **Answer (B) is incorrect** because Rule 1.8(d) prohibits a lawyer from acquiring literary rights to a client's story before the representation is concluded. **Answer (C) is incorrect** because the client is

indigent. There is no need to have the indigent client agree to repay the expenses under Rule 1.8(e)(2). **Answer (D) is incorrect** because some financial assistance to a client is permitted (although many types are not), and this happens to be among the types of assistance that the Rules permit. Answer (A) is correct.

19.   **The correct answer is (C).** As a former government lawyer, Jenna may not in private practice represent a client in a matter in which she was personally and substantially involved for the government without the government agency's informed consent. Rule 1.11(a)(2). She was personally and substantially involved in the Arbor road matter, and she would be representing the Chamber in that same matter. **Answer (A) is incorrect** because it does not matter which "side" she will be on. It is enough that she was personally and substantially involved in the matter while she represented the government agency. **Answer (B) is incorrect** because a lawyer can be personally and substantially involved without being lead counsel. **Answer (D) is incorrect** because informed consent of SDOT will cure the problem. Answer (C) is correct.

20.   **The correct answer is Answer (B). Answer (D) is incorrect** because it is possible in limited circumstances to obtain an enforceable advance waiver. However, Rule 1.8(h)(1) limits the lawyer's ability to make an agreement with a client prospectively limiting the lawyer's liability for malpractice. Because the interests of the lawyer and the client are so clearly at odds in such a negotiation, the client must have independent legal advice. **Answer (A) is incorrect** because Pamela's advice is not independent — it is her malpractice that would be waived. It is not enough for the client to give informed consent, or even to have the opportunity (but not the actuality) of independent counsel. Neither circumstance will ensure that the client makes a truly informed and fair decision. **Answer (C) is incorrect** because the mere opportunity for independent advice is not enough. The client must actually be independently represented in making the agreement. Answer (B), therefore, is correct.

21.   **The correct answer is Answer (A).** Kara has a personal interest conflict that will prevent her from being able to represent anyone like Wellington, who has been accused of a brutal sexual assault. However, this personal interest conflict will not be imputed to other lawyers in the firm, under Rule 1.10(a)(1). Therefore, other lawyers in the firm can undertake the representation. **Answer (B) is incorrect** because the personal interest conflict will not be imputed. **Answer (C) is incorrect** because screening is not necessary to prevent the imputation of the conflict. The nature of the conflict is such that it is automatically not imputed, even without screening. **Answer (D) is incorrect** because Kara cannot provide competent and diligent representation to Wellington. Therefore, her conflict is unconsentable under Rule 1.7(b)(1).

22.   **The correct answer is Answer (B).** It is not surprising that a long-time client might want to make a substantial gift to his trusted lawyer's daughter for her education. Because such gifts are not prohibited, **Answer (D) is incorrect.** Leah's problem is that she would be drafting an instrument for a client that benefited her child. She might not be able to render the independent professional judgment that Jacob is entitled to receive from his lawyer. **Answers (A) and (C), therefore, are incorrect,** because each would permit Leah to draft the will. She may not do so. Leah must tell Jacob that he can make the bequest but that another lawyer will have to draft the documents. Rule 1.8(c). Answer (B), therefore, is correct.

23. **The correct answer is Answer (A). Answer (C) is incorrect** because Hall's obligation is to her former client and not to the seller. Hall is tempted in this situation to use to her own advantage information she learned in the course of representing her former client. **Answer (D) is incorrect** because Hall has a continuing duty of confidentiality, even to a former client. There is a duty even to a client who discharged the lawyer, so **Answer (B) is also incorrect.** Under Rule 1.9(c)(1), Hall may not use the information to the disadvantage of her client unless the information has become generally known. Apparently, Hall's purpose is to buy the land cheap and sell it to her former client for a profit. That would be to the disadvantage of her former client. According to the question, the plans for the shopping center are still secret and therefore are not generally known. Her former client could, however, waive the requirements of Rule 1.9(c), although it is hard to imagine why the former client would do so in this case. Without that informed consent, Hall must not put her plan into effect. Answer (A) is correct.

24. **The correct answer is (B).** The lawyer has information relating to the representation but certainly could reasonably believe that revelation of the information is reasonably necessary to prevent reasonably certain death or substantial bodily injury to the victim. Therefore, under Rule 1.6(b)(1) the lawyer has the option but not the duty to reveal the information. **Answer (A) is incorrect** because the authority set forth in Rule 1.6(b)(1) is not a mandate; it is merely an option. **Answer (C) is incorrect** because the lawyer has an exception to the general rule of confidentiality, Rule 1.6(b)(1), whether or not the client consents. **Answer (D) is incorrect** because the lawyer is authorized to reveal the information even though it is confidential. Answer (B) is correct.

25. **The correct answer is (D).** Under Rule 1.2(d), a lawyer is prohibited from assisting a client with the perpetration of a fraud. Therefore, **Answers (B) and (C), both of which would permit the lawyer to render such assistance, are wrong. Answer (A) is wrong** because there are circumstances under which the lawyer may or even must tell the buyer about the fraud, even if the lawyer ceases his assistance once the fraud becomes known to the lawyer. If the buyer appears willing to proceed with the transaction even after the lawyer has refused to assist, the lawyer might reasonably believe that disclosure was reasonably necessary to prevent the substantial financial harm that will flow the client from the client's fraud, with which the lawyer has assisted. In that case, Rule 1.6(b)(2) would permit disclosure. It is even possible that the lawyer will be under a duty to disclose, if it is necessary to do so to avoid assisting in the fraud. Rule 4.1(b). Answer (D) is correct.

26. Jeremiah is a former client, and therefore the lawyer may undertake the new representation only if the two matters are not substantially related. Rule 1.9(a). The matters will be substantially related if, in the first representation, the lawyer would normally have learned confidential factual information that would materially the new client's position in the second matter. Comment 3 to Rule 1.9. Here, it is likely that the lawyer would have learned much about Jeremiah's driving and texting habits in the first case, and that information would materially advance the position of the new client, who is alleging that Jeremiah caused the accident. The lawyer could not undertake this new representation.

27. The lawyer needs to obtain informed consent of both clients to the conflict, under Rule 1.7(b)(4). In a joint representation, the lawyer must make sure that both clients understand that the lawyer's loyalty to one will be limited by the need to be loyal to the other, that the conversations that one client has with the lawyer will not be kept confidential from the other

client, that if disagreements develop between the clients the lawyer will have to withdraw from representing both (with added expense to both), and that it is likely that the attorney-client privilege will not protect conversations that one client has with the lawyer if litigation ensues between the clients. Comments 18, 30–32 to Rule 1.7.

28.   Matt represents an entity under Rule 1.13(a). He has learned that constituents of the corporation are engaged in illegal activities that are likely to be imputed to the company and are likely to cause substantial injury to the company. Matt's obligation, as the company's lawyer, is to proceed as reasonably necessary to protect the organization. In this circumstance the illegal activities are extremely serious, and therefore Matt will need to "report up," to tell his superiors about the situation and keep reporting up until someone acts to protect the company. This may include going all the way to the Board of Directors. Rule 1.13(b).

29.   Nina is obliged under Rule 1.8(g) to tell all of her clients the total amount of the aggregate settlement, the amount that each client is to receive, the amount of any attorney's fees or costs to be paid from the proceeds or by the opposing party, and the way in which any costs are to be apportioned among the clients. See ABA Formal Op. 06-438. Nina must also obtain the written informed consent of each client to the settlement. Rule 1.8(g).

30.   Yes, Sylvia should take affirmative steps to notify Millbank that Sylvia will no longer be the company's attorney. Comment 4 to Model Rule of Professional Conduct 1.4 notes that a client may assume that a lawyer who has rendered services for the client on a variety of matters over a substantial period of time will continue to act as the client's attorney. The lawyer should take steps to clarify the relationship so that the client will not "mistakenly suppose the lawyer is looking after the client's affairs when the lawyer has ceased to do so."

31.   The advance waiver will not be effective. Although advance waivers can be effective, especially when the client is a sophisticated consumer of legal services and is independently represented in agreeing to the waiver, the consent to this particular conflict is not effective because the conflict is non-consentable. See ABA Formal Op. 05-436. A conflict for one lawyer in the firm will be imputed to all members of the firm. Rule 1.10(a). The assertion of a claim in litigation is a "direct adversity" type of conflict under Rule 1.7(a), and Rule 1.7(b)(3) expressly makes consent to such a conflict impossible if the claims are being asserted against a client in the same suit in which the firm is representing the client. No consent, advance or not, would be effective as to this conflict.

32.   The lawyer may represent the son if the financial arrangements satisfy Rule 1.8(f) and the lawyer will be able to maintain independent professional judgment under Rule 5.4(c). The lawyer must obtain the son's consent for Osgood to pay the fee and must ensure that Osgood does not interfere with his professional judgment or expect him to share the son's confidential information with him. If these conditions are satisfied, the lawyer may represent the son and allow Osgood to pay his fee.

33.   Rene is right. Under these circumstances, Rene would be suing her client's insured. She would not be suing her client, and therefore she would not have a "direct adversity" type of conflict under Rule 1.7(a)(1). Rene may nevertheless have a conflict of interest, however. She will have a concurrent conflict if there is a significant risk that her representation of either

her new client or AIC will be materially limited by her responsibilities to the other. If that is the case, then Rene will have to determine whether the conflict is consentable and, if so, seek consent from both her new client and AIC. See Rule 1.7(b); ABA Formal Opinion 05-435.

34.   Abby does not have a conflict. Her representation of Nancy certainly would not be directly adverse to Herman, even though it will harm him, since Nancy is not asking Abby to litigate or negotiate against Herman. Because Nancy only wants Abby to do the ministerial act of rewriting the will to express her desire to disinherit Herman, there is no occasion for Abby to advise Nancy and thus no significant risk that his representation of Nancy will be materially limited by her responsibilities to Herman. See ABA Formal Op. 05-434.

TOPIC 2:   **ANSWERS**

COUNSELOR

35. **The correct answer is (B).** Lawyers are not under a general duty to offer unsolicited advice to clients, but here the client has instructed the lawyer to perform a task that will have serious adverse consequences for the client. See Comment 5 to Rule 2.1. The lawyer's obligation to communicate with the client under Rule 1.4(b) will require the lawyer to alert the client to the breach of contract. **Answer (A) is incorrect** because, although lawyers must not assist clients in the perpetration of a crime or fraud, there is nothing in the rules to prevent a lawyer from assisting with a mere breach of contract. **Answer (C) is wrong** because the lawyer has a duty to advise. **Answer (D) is wrong** because the lawyer is under no duty to follow the client's instructions. If the lawyer has a fundamental disagreement with the client or finds the client's proposed course of action to be repugnant, the lawyer may withdraw. Rule 1.16(b)(4).

36. **The correct answer is (B).** Under Rule 2.3, lawyers are generally permitted to provide an evaluation for a client to a third person, but only if doing so is compatible with other aspects of the lawyer's relationship with the client. Here, the lawyer's roles as advocate and as evaluator are fundamentally inconsistent, and the lawyer may not do both. See Comment 3 to Rule 2.3. **Answer (A) is incorrect** because informed consent is not enough if the evaluation is incompatible with the lawyer's other role as advocate. **Answer (C) is incorrect** because the key issue is not the effect on the client but the incompatible nature of the roles the lawyer is being asked to fulfill. An advocate simply has a different job than a dispassionate evaluator should have. Furthermore, the lawyer's report might well be discoverable by the opposing party — it is not privileged and it is not prepared in anticipation of litigation or preparation for trial — and even "favorable" evaluations could prove useful to an opposing party in litigation. **Answer (D) is wrong** because such a standard would make it impossible for a lawyer ever to prepare an evaluation for the use of third parties. Such evaluations are permitted as long as the requirements of Rule 2.3 are met.

37. **The correct answer is (D).** Under Rule 2.1, a lawyer may accept a request for technical legal advice at face value when the request comes from a sophisticated consumer of legal services like the general counsel for Monolith. See Comment 2 to Rule 2.1. **Answer (A) is incorrect** because sometimes lawyers may not take such requests at face value, such as when the request comes from a client who is inexperienced in legal matters. Id. **Answer (B) is incorrect** because the lawyer is free to give the requested technical legal advice to a sophisticated consumer of legal services. **Answer (C) is incorrect** because sometimes lawyers may give just technical legal advice, such as when a client like Monolith asks for it. Answer (D) is correct.

38. **The correct answer is Answer (A).** This is a rotten thing that Barbara wants to do, and to some it would be an immoral thing not to treat all the children fairly. Under Rule 2.1, lawyers are permitted but not required to counsel clients about the morality of their

proposed courses of action. **Answer (B) is incorrect** because such counseling is merely permitted and not required. **Answer (C) is incorrect** because Rule 2.1 allows lawyers to counsel clients about things other than the law, including questions of morality. **Answer (D) is incorrect** because the lawyer can assist with this transaction as long as it is not criminal or fraudulent. Lawyers are not prohibited from helping clients do legal but immoral things. Answer (A) is correct.

39.   **The correct answer is (B).** Under Rule 2.3, a lawyer who provides an evaluation for a client for use by third parties may or may not owe legal duties to the third parties. The existence and scope of any such duty is governed by other law and not the Rules of Professional Conduct. See Comment 3 to Rule 2.3. **Answer (D) is wrong** because there may be duties that arise under other law to third parties. **Answer (A) is wrong** because the Rules of Professional Conduct do not purport to impose the same duties a lawyer would owe a client on a lawyer performing an evaluation for third parties. **Answer (C) is incorrect** even though it correctly states that a lawyer cannot make a false statement of material fact to a third party. See Rule 4.1. Because other law may impose additional duties, however, Answer (C) is incomplete and therefore incorrect. Answer (B) is correct.

40.   Fernando's duty is to give his client the benefit of his independent professional judgment and candid advice. Here, the lawyer is obligated to deliver bad news, to have a very difficult discussion with the client. The lawyer's duty to give candid advice exists even if that advice is going to be unpalatable to the client. Comment 1 to Rule 2.1. Fernando may articulate his advice in the best way possible to maintain his client's morale, consistent with his duty to be truthful, but he cannot be dissuaded from giving his best advice just because the client is not going to like what she hears.

41.   John must tell his client that John will have to include in the opinion the limitations that the client placed upon his ability to investigate. See Comment 4 to Rule 2.3. The client is entitled to know that because the client has a decision to make: whether to allow John to continue, give John full disclosure, or to allow John to deliver a qualified report. See Rule 1.4(b). Even if this advice is not pleasing to the client, the lawyer is obliged to give it. See Comment 1 to Rule 2.1.

42.   **The correct answer is (A).** Generally, a lawyer may not be both a necessary witness in a case and also serve as an advocate in the case. However, there is an exception in Rule 3.7(a)(2) for cases like this one, in which the testimony will relate to the nature and value of the legal services rendered in the case. **Answer (B) is incorrect** because Cody need not withdraw. He may serve in both roles. **Answer (C) is incorrect** for the same reason. **Answer (D) is incorrect** because Cody's testimony relates only to the nature and value of legal services. The client need not forego recovery of attorney's fees just because the only witness who can establish their value is also the advocate in the case. Answer (A) is correct.

43.   **The correct answer is (D).** Rule 3.6 restricts what lawyers involved in an ongoing case may say publicly. Generally, they may not make statements that they know will be publicly disseminated (here, at a press conference) if there is a substantial likelihood that the statement will materially prejudice the case. Comment 5 to Rule 3.6 lists topics that are more likely than not to cause such prejudice, and among the items listed is the result of an examination or test. **Answer (A) is incorrect** because the First Amendment rights of lawyers are constrained by the need to provide to protect due process in the case. It should be tried in the courtroom and not in the press. **Answer (B) is incorrect** because this is not one of the statements listed in Rule 3.6(b), the list of "safe harbors." **Answer (C) is not correct** because it is overbroad. Lawyers involved in cases may make some statements. In particular, they can make the statements listed in the safe harbor provisions of Rule 3.6(b) and also make other statements, as long as there is not a substantial likelihood of materially prejudicing the case. Answer (D) is correct.

44.   **The correct answer is (A).** Under Rule 3.4(f), lawyers are permitted to ask some people, under some conditions, to refrain from voluntarily giving relevant information to another party. For that request to be proper, the person must be a relative or an employee or other agent of the lawyer's client, and the lawyer must reasonably believe that the person's interests will not be adversely affected by refraining from giving information voluntarily. Answer (A) is correct because this witness is not a relative, employee, or other agent. Therefore, the lawyer may not ask the witness not to talk to the other side's lawyer. **Answer (B) is incorrect** because it is overbroad. There are circumstances under which lawyers may ask witnesses not to give information voluntarily to another party. **Answer (C) is incorrect** because it satisfies only one of the two conditions that must be met before such a request is proper. The person must also be a relative, employee, or other agent of the client, and that is not true here. **Answer (D) is incorrect** because the status of former employee does not bring the witness within the circle of people whom the lawyer is permitted to ask to refrain from giving information voluntarily. The former employee is not a relative, employee, or other agent, and therefore the request is improper. Answer (A) is correct.

45.   **The correct answer is (C).** Under Rule 3.3(a)(3), a lawyer has the option to refuse to offer evidence, other than the evidence of a defendant in a criminal case, that the lawyer

reasonably believes is false. The girlfriend is not the client, and therefore Vickie has the option to call her or not. Vickie does not know for sure that the evidence will be false, but Vickie needs to have the option to refuse to call the girlfriend anyway to protect her efficacy as a trial lawyer. See Comment 9 to Rule 3.3. **Answer (D) is incorrect** because Vickie has the option to call the witness even if she reasonably believes the evidence will be false. **Answer (A) is incorrect** because Rule 3.3(a)(3) explicitly gives this decision to the lawyer, not the client. **Answer (B) is incorrect** because Vickie will not be violating the Rules of Professional Conduct whether she calls the witness or not. It is her option. Answer (C) is correct.

46.   **The correct answer is (A).** Because Deborah knows that a person has engaged in criminal conduct related to the proceeding, Deborah must take reasonable remedial measures including, if necessary, disclosure to the tribunal. Rule 3.3(b). **Answer (D) is incorrect** because the duty to act when criminal conduct has occurred is not contingent upon whether that conduct had the desired effect. **Answer (B) is incorrect** because, although this is information relating to the representation and thus otherwise protected by Rule 1.6, Rule 3.3(c) explicitly overrides the limitations of Rule 1.6 when the obligations of Rule 3.3(b) are triggered. **Answer (C) is incorrect** because Rule 3.3(b) requires action by the lawyer regardless of who has committed the criminal act related to the proceeding. Answer (A) is correct.

47.   **The correct answer is (B).** Under Rule 3.4(a), Amy must not counsel Fred to unlawfully destroy any item having potential evidentiary value. Amy must determine whether the destruction of the letters would be unlawful. For example, she may review the obstruction of justice statutes in the relevant jurisdiction. **Answer (A) is incorrect** because Amy may counsel Fred to destroy items of potential evidentiary value as long as the destruction is not unlawful under other law. **Answer (C) is incorrect** because it is possible that the letters have evidentiary value and that their destruction would be unlawful even before they are subpoenaed or requested. Some obstruction of justice statutes make it unlawful to destroy such evidence even before a proceeding is filed. **Answer (D) is incorrect** because Rule 3.4 forbids Amy from counseling Fred to engage in unlawful destruction of items having potential evidentiary value. She need not actually destroy, or assist in the destruction of, the documents. Answer (B) is correct.

48.   **The correct answer is (D).** Under Rule 3.5, a lawyer is not permitted to communicate with a juror if the juror has let the lawyer know that the juror does not want to communicate with the lawyer. **Answer (A) is incorrect** because violation of a court rule or court order is only one of the three circumstances that would bar the lawyer from communication with the juror. Any of the three alone will suffice. Similarly, **Answer (B) is incorrect** because it states only one of the three sets of circumstances under which the lawyer may not communicate with jurors. **Answer (C) is incorrect** because lawyers are permitted to speak to jurors unless one of the three conditions in Rule 3.5(c) is met. The blanket prohibition on contact is overbroad. Answer (D) is correct.

49.   **The correct answer is Answer (D).** Under Rule 3.1, a lawyer may not file a case that is frivolous, but a case that is unwarranted under existing law is nevertheless not frivolous if the lawyer can make a good faith argument for the extension, modification, or reversal of existing law. **Answer (A) is incorrect** because Gerald need not believe that he will win in order for the case not to be frivolous. See Comment 2 to Rule 3.1. **Answer (B) is incorrect**

because the case is not frivolous, even if there is authority directly on point to defeat it, if the lawyer has a good faith argument for the reversal of that precedent. **Answer (C) is incorrect** because the standard is good faith, not an objectively reasonable belief in a reasonable chance of winning. Answer (D) is correct.

50.   **The correct answer is Answer (C).** Under Rule 3.2, a lawyer has a duty to expedite litigation consistent with the legitimate interests of the client. However, as long as the lawyer has a substantial purpose for the continuance other than delay, seeking the continuance is proper. Here, the lawyer has such a purpose, to be with his ill father. **Answer (A) is incorrect** because the question is not just whether the client will benefit financially — an interest that will not by itself justify delay — but rather whether there is any substantial purpose for seeking the continuance other than delay. In this case, there is, for the lawyer to tend to his father. **Answer (B) is incorrect** because the lawyer's duty to expedite litigation is subject to exceptions. **Answer (D) is incorrect** because a client's financial interest in delay is not the kind of interest that legitimates a delay in litigation. See Comment 1 to Rule 3.2. Answer (C) is correct.

51.   **The correct answer is Answer (D).** Samuel is in a difficult situation. Ordinary social graces, with the added desire to be polite to the juror, may lead Samuel to speak to the juror. However, his duty under Rule 3.5(b) is clear: he must not have an ex parte communication with the juror without being authorized by law or by court order. Samuel must hope that the judge has made this obligation clear to the jurors so that they will not infer that lawyers in Samuel's position are being rude when they do not speak. With or without that protection, Samuel must not speak to the juror. **Answers (A), (B), and (C) are all incorrect** because they would authorize speaking to the juror without the necessary predicate of a law or court order.

52.   **The correct answer is Answer (A).** Lawyers have duties of candor to the courts, and under Rule 3.3(a)(2) the lawyer must sometimes disclose adverse legal authority to a tribunal. That duty exists, however, only if the authority is not disclosed by the opposing party. Here, the other lawyer disclosed it but simply did not make as much of it as Justin could have. Because the other lawyer disclosed it, Justin is under no obligation to do so. **Answers (B) and (C) are incorrect** because each states one of the other conditions that must be met before there is an obligation to disclose adverse authority: it is on point and from a controlling jurisdiction. Those two facts must both be true, and it must also be true that opposing counsel has not disclosed the authority, before the duty to disclose adverse authority arises. **Answer (D) is incorrect** because the Rules do not prohibit lawyers from choosing, as a strategic matter, to confront adverse legal authority or facts. A zealous advocate will sometimes do so to gain or preserve credibility with a court. Answer (A) is correct.

53.   **The correct answer is Answer (A).** Under Rule 3.4(b), a lawyer is prohibited from alluding in trial to any matter that the lawyer does not reasonably believe will be supported by admissible evidence. Good faith is not sufficient (and **Answer (B) is wrong**) because the test is objective, not subjective. The "nonfrivolous" standard mentioned in Answer (D) comes from Rule 3.1 dealing with meritorious claims and contentions. Because the standard is different at trial, **Answer (D) is wrong.** The standard is higher for statements made in trial because of the risk of causing a mistrial by putting evidence in front of the jury that, in the end, it should not have heard. On the other hand, it would be far too cumbersome to require a lawyer to obtain a prior ruling about every question of evidence. **Answer (C) is wrong** for

that reason. Glen merely needs a reasonable belief to justify mentioning the test in his opening statement. Answer (A) is correct.

54.   **The correct answer is Answer (B).** Under Rule 3.8(h), a prosecutor who has clear and convincing evidence that a defendant convicted in the prosecutor's jurisdiction was wrongfully convicted must seek to remedy the conviction by taking steps such as disclosing the evidence to the defendant, requesting that the court appoint counsel to represent an indigent defendant in this situation, and where appropriate, to notify the court that the defendant did not commit the offense. See Comment 9 to Rule 3.8. **Answer (A) is incorrect** because the prosecutor is a minister of justice and Rule 3.8(h) requires the prosecutor to act when the prosecutor has clear and convincing evidence that an injustice has been done. **Answers (C) and (D) are incorrect** because they do not go far enough. These are steps that a prosecutor must ordinarily take under Rule 3.8(g) when the prosecutor learns of credible and material evidence creating a reasonable likelihood that the defendant did not commit the crime for which the defendant was convicted. Where, as here, the prosecutor has more than that — clear and convincing evidence of innocence — the prosecutor must go further and seek to remedy the conviction.

55.   **The correct answer is Answer (A).** Under Rule 3.8(d), a prosecutor must make timely disclosure of all evidence that tends to negate guilt or mitigate the offense or that is mitigation evidence for sentencing. Here, the prosecutor has mitigation evidence for sentencing and must disclose it. **Answer (B) is incorrect** because the prosecutor's obligation of disclosure extends not just to information about guilt but also to evidence that mitigates the offense or would be mitigation evidence at the sentencing stage. **Answer (C) is incorrect** because prosecutors are ministers of justice and therefore have disclosure obligation that require the delivery of information and things that, for a civil lawyer, would be protected as work product. **Answer (D) is incorrect** because Rule 3.8(d) imposes the disclosure obligation without regard to the need for a request from the defendant. Answer (A) is correct.

56.   **The correct answer is Answer (D).** Stephen has a duty during the course of a proceeding not to put on false evidence and, if he discovers that false evidence has been offered, to take reasonable remedial measures. Rule 3.3(a)(3). Those remedial measures can include disclosure to the court despite the restrictions of Rule 1.6 on the disclosure of confidential information. Rule 3.3(c). However, once the proceeding is concluded, the lawyer has no duty under Rule 3.3 to disclose the false evidence to the court. Rule 3.3(a)(3). **Answers (A) and (C), both of which would require the lawyer to reveal the information, are therefore incorrect.** The purpose of this limitation is to place some practical limit on the lawyer's obligation to rectify false evidence. Comment 13 to Rule 3.3. It has nothing to do with the protection of confidentiality. If the case was still pending, the lawyer would have to reveal the perjury if his client would not. **Answer (B), therefore, is incorrect.** Stephen need not disclose the perjury because the proceeding has concluded. Answer (D) is correct.

57.   Shelley has the duty to institute reasonable remedial measures. Under Rule 3.3(a)(3), she may not offer evidence that she knows to be false. This includes the deposition testimony of her client. Comment 1 to Rule 3.3. Reasonable remedial measures include trying to talk the client into correcting the record and, if that fails, seeking to withdraw if that would cure the problem. It is hard to imagine how withdrawal in this situation would cure the problem, so if Shelley's client will not correct the record Shelley will need to go to the next step, disclosure

to the tribunal. See Comment 10 to Rule 3.3.

58. As a subordinate lawyer, Victor is bound to comply with the Rules of Professional Conduct but may rely on a superior's reasonable resolution of an arguable question of professional duty. Rule 5.2. Under Rule 3.4(b), Victor may not offer the witness an inducement that is prohibited by law, and the common law rule in most jurisdictions is that a lawyer may not pay a contingent fee to an expert. Victor must decide if his superior's instruction is a reasonable resolution of an arguable question of professional duty and must consider such questions as whether this arrangement is really a contingent fee and, if so, whether the rule in Victor's jurisdiction is any different from the common law rule.

59. Under Rule 3.4(a), an attorney is not permitted to unlawfully alter material having potential evidentiary value. If there is a law that would reach this evidence, such as an obstruction of justice statute (as there likely would be), then the attorney must be careful that the gun is not "altered" in any material way by the testing. If it is not, and if the lawyer turns the gun over in a timely manner, then the lawyer does not run the risk of having "unlawfully altered" the evidence.

60. Linda may file this case even though there has never been such a case before. Rule 3.1 forbids Linda from filing any "frivolous" cases, but it is not frivolous to file a case that argues in good faith for the extension of existing law. The existing law of assault and battery presumably would allow for recovery of damages from people who bully others physically and cause harm, and this case would be an attempt to extend that doctrine to virtual bullying. The case therefore would not be frivolous under Rule 3.1, and Linda may file it.

61. Penny's client has committed fraud that relates to the proceeding. Penny has the obligation, therefore, to undertake reasonable remedial measures, including if necessary disclosure of the fraud to the tribunal. Rule 3.3(b). If the client will not correct the record, and if withdrawal either will not be permitted or would not cure the problem (as is likely), then Penny is going to have to tell the court. See Comment 10 to Rule 3.3 (describing reasonable remedial measures).

62. **The correct answer is (C).** Lawyers are not allowed under Rule 4.1 to make false statements of material fact to third persons. However, statements of value are not relied on in our culture as statements of fact. Instead, under generally accepted practices in negotiation, it is expected that each side will "puff" about value. See Comment 1 to Rule 4.1. Rosemary, therefore, may state the inflated value of the property. **Answer (A) is incorrect** because the general rule against making false statements of fact does not apply to statements of value. **Answer (B) is incorrect** because lawyers are constrained by Rule 4.1 not to make material misstatements of fact even outside of a court proceeding. **Answer (D) is incorrect** because there is no duty to disclose the appraisal. Under Rule 4.1(b), Rosemary would have the obligation to reveal material information like the appraisal only if it was necessary in order to avoid assisting in a fraud. Answer (C) is correct.

63. **The correct answer is (A).** Under Rule 1.2(d), Clarence may not assist the client in the perpetration of a fraud. Clarence must withdraw because otherwise he will violate Rule 1.2(d). See Rule 1.16(a). Therefore, **Answer (D) is incorrect. Answer (B) is incorrect** because Clarence at least has the option to inform the buyers to prevent the significant financial harm that otherwise will befall the buyers in a fraudulent transaction in which the client has used the lawyer's services. Rule 1.6(b)(2). If disclosure is necessary to avoid assisting in the fraud, Clarence has the obligation and not just the option to inform the buyers of the fraud. Rule 4.1(b). Therefore, **Answer (C) is incorrect** because it states that disclosure is optional even when it is necessary to avoid assisting in fraud. Answer (A) most accurately states Clarence's responsibilities.

64. **The correct answer is (A).** Wilco has the right to inspect and copy company e-mails. Because these messages were not "inadvertently sent," Randy has no obligation under Rule 4.4(b) to notify opposing counsel that he has them, unless rules of civil procedure or other law impose that duty. See ABA Formal Op. 11-460. **Answer (B) is incorrect** because it states the duty under Rule 4.4(b), which does not apply. **Answer (C) is incorrect** because there is no duty under the Model Rules of Professional Conduct to notify or send, although rules of procedure or other law could impose such a duty. **Answer (D) is incorrect** because Randy has not violated Rule 4.4(a)'s prohibition on obtaining evidence in violation of the rights of third person's. Randy did not gather the evidence, and in any event Wilco was within its rights to obtain the messages. Furthermore, even if Randy had violated a Rule, that would not require him to seek to withdraw (although that might be a remedy sought by the plaintiff if Randy had obtained evidence in violation of her rights). Answer (A) is correct.

65. **The correct answer is Answer (C).** Ramon will cause embarrassment with this evidence, and he would violate Rule 4.4(a) if he had no substantial purpose other than that. In this case, however, the husband's drug use and other odd behavior is surely relevant to the issue of custody, and so Ramon has the substantial purpose of showing that his client will provide a better environment for the children. As long as he has such a substantial purpose, he may

use means that cause embarrassment. **Answer (A) is incorrect** because lawyers cannot use even legal means that have no substantial purpose other than to cause embarrassment. **Answer (B) is incorrect** because the standard is whether the lawyer has any substantial purpose other than the embarrassment. Parties to litigation are embarrassed regularly about probative evidence against them. Their embarrassment by itself does not prevent lawyers from using such evidence to help their clients. **Answer (D) is wrong** because mixed motives are acceptable. Ramon need not demonstrate that he has no purpose other than the legitimate one of showing that the husband would not be a suitable custodial parent. As long as Ramon has that legitimate purpose, the husband's embarrassment is no bar to use of the evidence. Answer (C) is correct.

66. **The correct answer is Answer (D).** Under Rule 4.1(a), lawyers are prohibited from making false statements of law, which is exactly what Brian has done. Under Rule 8.4(a), that violation of Rule 4.1(a) is misconduct. **Answer (A) is incorrect** because it is the making of the statement that is the violation, not the reasonableness of anyone's reliance on it. That issue might matter under the substantive law of fraud, but it is not relevant to the violation of Rule 4.1(a). **Answer (B) is incorrect** because misstatements of law are violations of Rule 4.1(a), not just misstatements of fact. **Answer (C) is incorrect** because Rule 4.1(a) is not triggered by disparity in experience or knowledge. Any material misstatement of the law, even among lawyers of equal experience and knowledge, is a violation of Rule 4.1(a). Answer (D) is correct.

67. **The correct answer is Answer (B).** Lawyers are permitted to have direct contact with former constituents of a represented organization. See Comment 7 to Rule 4.2. Therefore, there was nothing wrong with having the contact. However, lawyers must not use means of obtaining evidence that violate the rights of third persons, and using a disgruntled former employee to obtain privileged documents violates the rights of the drug company to the privilege. **Answer (A) is wrong** because the direct contact was permissible. **Answer (C) is wrong** on all counts. The contact is permitted but obtaining the evidence is not. This answer reverses those conclusions. **Answer (D) is wrong** because one part of Victoria's acts is misconduct. Answer (B) is correct.

68. **The correct answer is Answer (C).** When a lawyer knows that an opposing party is represented in the matter, the lawyer may not have direct contact with that opposing party without permission of the other party's lawyer. Rule 4.2. However, when the opposing party is an organization, the lawyer may have direct contact with constituents of the organization as long as the constituent does not fall into any one of three categories. This loading dock worker presumably does not regularly consult with GEI's lawyers about the matter or have the authority to bind the company in the matter. It is given in the question that he did not cause the accident, so no act or omission of his will be attributed to the organization for purposes of civil liability. Deanna, therefore, may talk to the employee without permission of GEI's lawyer. **Answer (A) is incorrect** because the obligations of Rule 4.2 are not dependent in any way upon whether there is pending litigation. **Answer (B) is wrong** because the loading dock worker does not fit into any of the categories of corporate constituents who are off-limits. **Answer (D) is incorrect** because current employees or other current constituents may be contacted without permission of GEI's lawyers as long as they do not fit into any of the three categories of people who are off-limits. Answer (C) is correct.

69. **The correct answer is Answer (D).** Clients like Sandy sometimes get impatient with their

own lawyers and contact their adversary's lawyers directly. By doing so, Sandy creates a problem for Lawrence because he is bound by Rule 4.2 not to have direct contact with a represented party, even one who consents and who is angry at her own lawyer. Lawrence must immediately terminate the conversation. Comment 3 to Rule 4.2. **Answers (A), (B), and (C) are incorrect** because they would permit Lawrence to continue the conversation. He must terminate it. The best practice would then be to notify Sandy's counsel of the contact, but under no circumstances may Lawrence continue the conversation with a represented party. Answer (D) is correct.

70. **The correct answer is Answer (A).** No Rule of Professional Conduct directly bars Krista from counseling the client to tape the conversation. **Answer (D) is incorrect** because the ABA has concluded that taping conversations is not inherently deceitful. ABA Formal Op. 01-422. Because it is not a crime in every jurisdiction for one party to a conversation to tape it, **Answer (C) is incorrect.** However, in some states it is a crime to tape a conversation without the consent of all parties. A lawyer in such a jurisdiction could not tape because the lawyer would be committing a criminal act that reflects adversely on the attorney's honesty and trustworthiness, in violation of Rule 8.4(b). If the lawyer cannot do the taping, then Krista may not use the client as her agent to violate the Rules of Professional Conduct. Rule 8.4(a). **Answer (B) is incorrect** because Krista may not escape any culpability just by having her client do the taping. Krista must check the law of her local jurisdiction before counseling her client to wear a wire.

71. **The correct answer is (D).** Under Rule 1.2(d), Stanley may not assist in the perpetration of a fraud. When continued representation will require the lawyer to violate the Rules of Professional Conduct, the lawyer must withdraw. Rule 1.16(a)(1). **Answers (A) and (C) are incorrect** because withdrawal is mandatory, not permissive. The harder part of the question concerns notice to the banks. Stanley must make sure that he avoids assisting in the fraud, and he may give notice of his withdrawal to the banks if his withdrawal is not enough. This is the so-called "noisy withdrawal." See Comment 10 to Rule 1.2 and Comment 3 to Rule 4.1. **Answer (B) is incorrect** because Stanley has this option. The noisy withdrawal is not a mandatory step, however, because under Rule 1.6(b)(2) Stanley would have the option to reveal the fraud to the banks, thus making the "noisy withdrawal" unnecessary. The "noisy withdrawal" is simply an interim step that a lawyer might take to avoid assisting in the fraud without going so far as to reveal confidential client information. Answer (D) is correct because the withdrawal is mandatory but the notice of the withdrawal to the banks is simply one option.

72. Ralph may access the "meta-data." There is nothing in the Model Rules of Professional Conduct to prevent him from doing so. Nothing in the question indicates that Ralph would be using methods to obtain evidence that violate the rights of third parties. See Rule 4.4(a). After all, this information was produced to him, and in any event the comments and changes were not made by counsel. Although it is possible that his opposing counsel could have taken steps to "scrub" the "meta-data" from the electronic version of the document, Ralph is under no obligation to decline to look for it. See ABA Formal Op. 06-442.

73. Yes, Joy's plan is consistent with her obligations under the Model Rules of Professional Conduct. The tension here arises from Joy's responsibility not to have contact with the husband, whom she knows to be represented by counsel. See Rule 4.2. Although Joy has no intention of doing so directly, she is thinking about suggesting that her client do so. Joy of

course cannot violate the rules herself or through the acts of another. Rule 8.4(a). On the other hand, clients have the right to speak to each other, and Joy owes her client a duty of candid advice under Rule 2.1. See Comment 4 to Rule 4.2. This tension has been resolved in favor of permitting the lawyer to suggest to the client that the client may contact the opposing party directly, and the lawyer may even coach the client about how to approach and negotiate with the represented party on the other side. ABA Formal Op. 11-461.

74.   Dayle may bluff about her settlement authority. Under Rule 4.1, she is not permitted to make material misstatements of fact. Statements about the acceptability of a certain sum in settlement of a matter generally speaking are not statements of fact. Comment 2 to Rule 4.1. The fact that the negotiation is being conducted as a caucus negotiation does not change the attorney's responsibilities or options. ABA Formal Op. 06-439.

75. **The correct answer is (B).** This is a question of multijurisdictional practice under Rule 5.5. As an in-house counsel, Jack may work on a permanent basis in a state where he is not licensed as long as his services do not include services for which the forum requires pro hac vice admission (i.e., as long as they are not court appearances). Rule 5.5(d)(1). Answer (B) correctly identifies the problem: with this job description, Jack would be representing the company in court in his new state with a license from another state. **Answer (A) is incorrect** because Jack is permitted under Rule 5.5(d)(1) to practice law as an in-house counsel in the new state as long as he is not appearing in court. His counseling about "bad faith," for example, is the practice of law in a state where he is not licensed but is permissible. **Answer (C) is incorrect** because it is overbroad. His status as in-house counsel is significant because it permits him to do some activities without a local license, but it does not permit the court appearances that will be in his job description. **Answer (D) is incorrect** because a license in one state does not carry the unqualified right to practice in another state. U.S. lawyers are still licensed and regulated on a state-by-state basis and, under the Model Rules of Professional Conduct, may undertake legal activities in a state where they are not licensed only in the limited circumstances set forth in Rule 5.5.

76. **The correct answer is (A).** Under Rule 5.6(b), lawyers are not permitted to offer or make agreements that restrict the lawyer's right to practice. This provision is a covenant not to compete, and it would restrict Irene's right to practice and thus deprive the public of the availability of her services. Only Answer (A) correctly states that Irene may not make this agreement. **Answers (B), (C), and (D) are all incorrect** because those answers make this impermissible agreement permissible, at least under certain conditions. Answer (A) is correct.

77. **The correct answer is (B).** The general rule is that a lawyer cannot share legal fees with a nonlawyer. Rule 5.4(a). One of the exceptions, however, permits lawyers like Carl to share court-ordered legal fees with a nonprofit organization that employs, retains, or recommends the lawyer in the matter. Rule 5.4(a)(4). Answer (B) is therefore correct. **Answers (A) and (D) are incorrect** because of the exception in Rule 5.4(a)(4). **Answer (C) is wrong** because the employer must be nonprofit before the lawyer can share fees. Answer (B) is correct.

78. **The correct answer is Answer (C).** Under Rule 5.5(c)(4), a lawyer licensed in one state may provide services in other states on a temporary basis as long as those services are not related to litigation of alternative dispute resolution and as long as they arise out of or are reasonably related to the lawyer's practice in her home state. Here, Laurie is just giving advice, so these activities are not related to litigation or alternative dispute resolution. This is what she does at home and elsewhere, so the out-of-state activities relate to her home state practice. **Answer (A) is incorrect** because these are authorized temporary activities. **Answer (B) is incorrect** because it does not matter whether Laurie is advising about federal law. As long as her non-litigation, non-ADR activities arise out of or are reasonably

related to her home practice, federal or not, the activities are permitted. **Answer (D) is incorrect** because pro hac vice admission is for litigation. Laurie is not participating in litigation. Because she is just giving advice, pro hac vice admission is unnecessary.

79. **The correct answer is Answer (C).** Nick could sell all of his practice by complying with Rule 1.17's requirements regarding notice to existing clients and other matters. **Answer (A) is wrong** because it is possible, under the right circumstances, to sell a law practice. Because Nick also has the option of selling an entire area of practice, such as the estate planning portion of the practice, Rule 1.17(b), **Answer (B) (must sell all or nothing) is incorrect.** A partial sale would enable him to stay in practice but scale back his activities. See Comment 5 to Rule 1.17. Nick then would not be permitted to undertake representation in the estate planning field. What he cannot do is sell a portion of an area of practice without selling all of that portion of his practice. **Answer (D), therefore, is incorrect.** The purpose of this restriction is to prevent lawyers from selling off less lucrative clients who might have trouble obtaining other counsel. Comment 6 to Rule 1.16. Answer (C) is correct.

80. **The correct answer is Answer (D).** It is possible that this is a false and misleading communication, because it may create unjustified expectations that Dane can accomplish the same results for others without regard to the underlying merits of their claims. See Comment 3 to Rule 7.1. This question raises the issue of vicarious liability for the actions of nonlawyer assistants. Under Rule 5.3, Dane will be responsible if he orders or ratifies the conduct, or if he fails to take remedial action at a time when the consequences could be avoided (for example, by sending out a follow-up message: "I cant guarantee the same results 4 u — all cases r different!"). **Answer (A) is incorrect** because Rule 5.3(c) lists the circumstances under which a lawyer can be responsible, as a disciplinary matter, for actions of nonlawyer assistants. **Answers (B) and (C) refer to two of the circumstances under which there will be such liability, but these answers are incorrect** because these are not the only such circumstances. Answer (D) is correct.

81. **The correct answer is Answer (D).** Under Rule 5.5, Doug may conduct some temporary activities in another state, but he may not establish an office there, represent to the public that he is licensed to practice there, or practice there on a continuous and systematic basis. Here, Doug "regularly" goes into the adjoining state to meet and service clients. That continuous and systematic presence violates Rule 5.5. **Answers (A) and (B) are incorrect** because the establishment of an office and misrepresentation of licensure are two of the grounds for finding misconduct, but they are not the only ones. **Answer (C) is incorrect** because it is too general. Under Rule 5.5, lawyers are authorized under the right circumstances to practice law in another state. The problem for Doug, of course, is that he does not fit any of those circumstances. Answer (D) is correct.

82. **The correct answer is Answer (D).** Temporary activities in a state where a lawyer is not licensed are governed by Rule 5.5. Because not all temporary activities are permitted, **Answer (A) is wrong.** Usually, litigation-related activities require admission pro hac vice by the court in the other state. Answer (C) states the standard for non-litigation temporary activities, but witness interviews are related to litigation. **Answer (C), therefore, is incorrect.** Harry's problem is that he cannot be admitted pro hac vice to the court until the case is filed. He may need to interview these witnesses to decide whether he is permitted to file the case at all. See Federal Rule of Civil Procedure 11. To classify these pre-filing activities as improper would be to place lawyers like Harry potentially in a Catch-22

situation. For that reason, Rule 5.5(c)(2) permits Harry to proceed as long as the interviews are reasonably related to a potential proceeding in which he reasonably expects to be authorized by the court to proceed. **Answer (B) is incorrect** because it would create the Catch-22. Answer (D) is correct.

83. **The correct answer is Answer (B).** Amber may not make an offer to settle a case that includes a restriction on the other lawyer's right to practice. Rule 5.6(b). If the client insists, then Amber will have to withdraw under Rule 1.16(a)(1). However, there is an intermediate step. The client may not know that this is something the lawyer cannot do, and therefore Amber must consult with the client under Rule 1.4(a)(5) about the limitation on her conduct. **Answer (A) is incorrect** because Amber would be committing misconduct even by making such an offer. **Answer (C) is incorrect** because Amber must consult with the client about the limitations on her conduct before abruptly withdrawing. **Answer (D) is correct** in that Amber must consult, but it is incorrect in describing the consultation. This is not a run-of-the-mill consultation about means. It is instead a communication from the lawyer that the lawyer cannot do something the client has asked her to do. Answer (B) is correct.

84. **The correct answer is (B).** Keith must be careful not to practice law in a jurisdiction where he is not authorized to do so. Under Rule 5.5, Keith could represent a client in an alternative dispute resolution proceeding on a temporary basis in another state if the mediation arose out of or was reasonably related to his practice. It is neither, and so Keith must look for some other authorization to help. Answer (B) is correct because the only authorization available to him is Rule 5.5(c)(1), which authorizes lawyers to practice temporarily in another jurisdiction as long as they associate local counsel and that counsel is active in the matter. **Answer (A) is incorrect** because this mediation does not arise out of or reasonably relate to Keith's practice, so Rule 5.5(c)(3) will not authorize his help. **Answer (C) is incorrect** because there is an alternative, to associate the local lawyer. **Answer (D) is incorrect** because there are numerous circumstances under which lawyers may practice law temporarily in jurisdictions where they are not licensed. Answer (B) is correct.

85. Melody has no choice but to request that the court not assign her any more cases until her circumstances are such that she can competently and diligently represent her clients. All clients, including those whose lawyers are appointed by the court and paid by the state, are entitled to competent and diligent counsel. If Melody undertakes more cases, she will be violating her duties under Rules 1.1 (competence) and 1.3 (diligence). See ABA Formal Op. 06-441.

86. Rita is obligated not to seek to avoid the appointment unless good cause exists. Rule 6.2. One example of good cause is when the representation is likely to result in a violation of the Rules of Professional Conduct. Here, it is likely that Rita has a conflict of interest in representing this defendant. Lawyers and clients often develop good relationships, and Rita may have a hard time representing the alleged killer of her former client without being materially limited by her feelings for the victim. If that is the case, then Rita would be obliged to seek to avoid this appointment.

87. The "retirement plan" is not consistent with the Model Rules of Professional Conduct. Generally, lawyers are not permitted to enter into covenants not to compete. See Rule 5.6(a). An exception to this rule is an agreement concerning benefits upon retirement, but the proposed plan is a "retirement plan" in name only. It is not limited to lawyers of a certain

age or after a certain number of years of service, and the "benefits" are amounts that are already owed to the lawyers. In effect, the agreement is nothing more than an agreement not to compete, on pain of forfeiture of sums that belong to the departing lawyer. That is not a "retirement plan," and it would violate Rule 5.6(a). See ABA Formal Op. 06-444.

88.   Penny should be concerned first that she would be in violation of Rule 5.5(a) because she would be assisting in the unauthorized practice of law. Costco, Inc. is not licensed to practice law, and by offering legal services through its own salaried employees, for a profit, Costco might be found to be engaging in the unauthorized practice of law. At the very least, Penny should be worried about her independence. She would be serving individual clients, but she would be paid and supervised by employees of Costco. Under Rule 5.4(c), Penny must be careful to make sure that her employer does not purport to direct or regulate her professional judgment in representing the members.

89.   Reggie may not follow the partner's instructions. Reggie is a subordinate lawyer, but he is bound by the Rules of Professional Conduct. Rule 5.2(a). He has a defense to misconduct based upon his superior's instructions only if those instructions reflect a reasonable resolution of an arguable question of professional duty. Rule 5.2(b). The partner has instructed Reggie to engage in a clear violation of Rule 3.3(d), which requires lawyers in an ex parte proceeding to reveal all material facts that will help the court make an informed decision, regardless of whether those facts are adverse to the lawyer's client. Reggie will commit misconduct if he follows the partner's instructions.

90.   **The correct answer is (C).** Louise has been appointed by the court to represent this defendant. Under Rule 6.2, she may not seek to avoid the appointment unless she has good cause. The only statement of the four that would constitute good cause is Answer (C), because if she represents the defendant without the competence to do so then she is violating Rule 1.1 (and inviting reversal of any conviction for ineffective assistance of counsel). **Answer (A) is incorrect** and indeed irrelevant because this is not pro bono representation. Louise is being paid for the work, and she has been appointed to do it by the court. **Answer (B) is incorrect** because only an unreasonable financial burden will constitute good cause. **Answer (D) is incorrect** because the political beliefs of the lawyer are irrelevant unless the lawyer's representation of the client is likely to be impaired. Mere belief in law and order does not necessarily mean that a lawyer would be impaired in representing a criminal defendant. Answer (C) is correct.

91.   **The correct answer is Answer (A).** No court has appointed Miriam, so she is free to decline to represent this client for any reason, including his patronizing comment. **Answer (B) is incorrect** because that is the standard for seeking to avoid court appointments, but that is not what happened here. **Answer (C) is incorrect** because Miriam does not have to undertake this representation even if the relationship is great, much less impaired. In the absence of a court appointment, she is free to choose her clients. **Answer (D) is incorrect** because lawyers are constrained to accept particular engagements only when they are court appointed, and even then the lawyers may seek to avoid the appointment under the right circumstances. Answer (A) is correct.

92.   **The correct answer is (C).** Under Rule 6.1, pro bono work and contributions to organizations that provide legal services to people of limited means are strongly encouraged but not required. One way in which the Rule encourages pro bono service is the statement that Answer (C) quotes verbatim. That would be a legitimate argument using the Model Rules. **Answers (A), (B), and (D) are all incorrect** because they are misrepresentations of the requirements of the Model Rules. None of them are true under the Model Rules. Answer (C) is correct.

93.   **The correct answer is (B).** Under Rule 6.3, a lawyer like Eugene may serve as a director of a legal services organization even if the lawyer's firm and the people served by the organization have differing interests. The lawyer's responsibility is not to participate in an action or a decision of the organization if doing so would create a conflict with a client of the lawyer under Rule 1.7 or if the decision or action could have a material adverse effect on the client of the legal services organization, if that client has interests adverse to a client of the lawyer. Rule 6.3(a) and (b). Answer (B) is therefore correct that Eugene may not participate in any decisions regarding the claim against the hospital. **Answers (A) and (D) are incorrect** because they require more action that Rule 6.3 requires. **Answer (C) is incorrect** because Eugene does not have the option to participate in the decisions of the organization

on this matter given the conflict between the people being served by the organization and his firm's client.

94.   **The correct answer is Answer (A).** With or without any certification as a specialist, a lawyer can always under Rule 7.4(a) advertise that the lawyer does or does not practice in particular fields of law. **Answers (B), (C), and (D), however, are incorrect** because Joshua is not permitted to advertise this certification as a specialist. To be entitled to do that, the certifying organization would have to be approved by an appropriate state authority or accredited by the ABA, and the advertisement would need to include the name of the Institute. Here, the Institute has not been approved by anyone, and so the lawyer may not advertise a specialty based upon a certification from the Institute. Answer (A) is correct.

95.   **The correct answer is (A).** Wayne is giving something of value to the friend in exchange for sending him business, and that violates Rule 7.2(b). Even if the $1000 fee really is for writing advertisements — and one must be skeptical of that characterization of the arrangement — the facts make it clear that the friend receives the valuable opportunity to write the ad for a fee only because of the referral. At the very least, Wayne would be giving that bit of value for the referral, and that is a violation. **Answer (B) is incorrect** because client consent is not relevant to a violation of Rule 7.2(b). The clients should never have been steered to Wayne by such an arrangement in the first place. **Answer (C) is incorrect** because Wayne is not just paying for advertising in the normal course of business. He is engaging in a quid pro quo — the friend sends business and in exchange the friend gets to do the advertising. **Answer (D) is incorrect** because exclusivity only matters to a reciprocal referral arrangement not otherwise prohibited by the rules. This is not a reciprocal referral arrangement, such as one between Wayne and the chiropractor. Furthermore, the arrangement does otherwise violate the rule because of the value that Wayne is giving for the referrals. Answer (A) is correct.

96.   **The correct answer is (C).** Lawyers may not solicit clients when a significant motive for the lawyer doing so is pecuniary gain, with some exceptions that do not apply here. Rule 7.3(a). Cathy is trying to set precedent, but she needs the money. The fee is therefore a significant motive for the solicitation and it is not allowed. If she was motivated solely by the desire to set a precedent or by other reasons that had nothing to do with money, then she could solicit. **Answer (A) is incorrect** because it is enough for pecuniary concerns to be a significant motivation. They need not be the only motivation. **Answer (B) is incorrect** because what matters is the motivation, not the type of case. **Answer (D) is incorrect** because there are circumstances under which lawyers can solicit prospective clients who are not existing clients, although the solicitation of existing clients is allowed. Answer (C) is correct.

97.   **The correct answer is (B).** This particular advertisement comes dangerously close to stating that clients should hire Scott because he will have influence with the judge. Indeed, it is hard to imagine why else the lawyer would want to advertise his role in the judge's campaign. An advertisement that stated truthfully that the lawyer could obtain results by trading on his relationship with the judge would violate Rule 8.4(e). This advertisement, which implies the same thing, also violates that Rule even though the influence is merely

implied. See also Comment 4 to Rule 7.1. Answer (B), therefore, is correct. **Answer (A) is incorrect** because the Model Rules do not purport to regulate good taste in advertising. See Comment 3 to Rule 7.2. **Answer (C) is incorrect** because the judge's permission is irrelevant if the message is that the lawyer has inappropriate influence. **Answer (D) is incorrect** because it is not always enough for an advertisement to be true.

98. **The correct answer is Answer (C).** With only a few exceptions, lawyers are not allowed to solicit employment face-to-face, by live telephone contact, or through real-time electronic communication. A text message, unlike for example a "live chat" over the internet, is not a real-time electronic communication. Like an e-mail or a letter, a text message does not require an immediate response. Therefore, lawyers may solicit by text just as they could by letter, as long as the message contains the words "advertising material" at the beginning and end of each message to someone other than Judy's close personal friends. **Answer (A) is incorrect** because it states the general rule for lawyer communications rather than the specific rule dealing with solicitation. **Answer (B) is incorrect** because this is not a real-time electronic contact and therefore Judy is not limited to contacting only close personal friends. **Answer (D) is incorrect** for the same reason. Answer (C) is correct.

99. **The correct answer is Answer (A).** The proposal would be a written solicitation of work, which normally would require the warning to the recipient that it is "advertising material." However, no such warning is necessary because the recipient asked to receive the proposal. Comment 7 to Rule 7.3. **Answer (B) is incorrect** because "advertising material" need not be included on the outside of the envelope of a response to a request for information from a potential client. **Answer (C) is incorrect** because it states one of the circumstances under which a face-to-face, live telephone, or real-time electronic solicitation would be permitted. This response to the request is not such a solicitation. **Answer (D) is incorrect** because it too relates to one of the circumstances that makes face-to-face, live telephone, or real-time electronic solicitation improper. Since the response to the FDIC's request is none of these, Answer (D) is inapposite. Answer (A) is correct.

100. **The correct answer is Answer (A).** Trade names for law firms are permissible (so Answer (C) is wrong), but the potential problem with this one is that it might create confusion. In particular, by calling it the "Centerville Legal Clinic," the lawyer may be creating the impression that his law office is a public legal aid agency. Joe may use the trade name if he guards against that mistake by including a disclaimer that makes it clear that his practice is not a public legal aid agency. See Comment 1 to Rule 7.5. **Answers (B) and (D) would not provide that protection and are, therefore, incorrect.** Answer (A) is correct.

101. **The correct answer is (B).** Under Rule 7.6, the firm cannot accept the appointment if it made political contributions for the purpose of obtaining or being considered for the contract to be the county defender. **Answer (A) is incorrect** because the contributions in and of themselves are not improper. They raise an issue under Rule 7.6 only if they were made for the purpose of obtaining or being considered for the contract. **Answer (C) is incorrect** because the contributions can be improper even if they do not constitute a crime, although of course if they are criminal then Rule 8.4(b) comes into play. See Comment 6 to Rule 7.6. **Answer (D) is incorrect** because Rule 7.6 may not permit the firm to accept the contract if the contributions were made for the wrong reasons. Answer (B) is correct.

102. **The correct answer is (C).** Under Rule 7.5(d), lawyers may not state or imply that they

practice as a partnership or other organization if that is not true. Here, these lawyers are both solo practitioners, but use of the name "Chapman & McCain" would imply that they are a partnership. **Answer (A) is incorrect** because it is not enough to share office space. If the lawyers do not practice as part of the same organization, they may not imply that they do. **Answer (B) is incorrect** because it is irrelevant that the lawyers are using their real names. The problem is the implication that they practice as part of an organization when in truth they do not. **Answer (D) is incorrect** because it would permit a form of "bait and switch." The firm name may attract clients because it implies that this is a law firm — indeed, that is one of the reasons the lawyers want to use it — and it would be unfair and deceptive to allow clients to come to them for that reason only to be told that, after all, the lawyers do not practice as a firm. Answer (C) is correct.

103. **The correct answer is (A).** Under Rule 7.3(d), a lawyer does not violate the anti-solicitation provisions of Rule 7.3(a) just because the lawyer participates in a prepaid legal services plan, as long as certain conditions are met. **Answer (B), therefore, is incorrect. Answer (C) is incorrect**, even though it correctly states one of the conditions that must be satisfied under Rule 7.3(d). Even if the lawyer does not own or operate the plan (and here the attorney clearly does not), the Rule would be violated if the plan was soliciting people who were known to be in need of particular legal services covered by the plan. **Answer (D) is incorrect** because an attorney can commit misconduct through the acts of another. See Rule 8.4(a). It is not enough to say that the attorney was not personally involved. Answer (A) is correct.

104. **The correct answer is (B).** Under Rule 7.2(b), a lawyer is prohibited from giving anything of value in exchange for recommending the lawyer's services, with certain exceptions. One of those exceptions is that an attorney may pay the usual charges of an attorney referral service if the service is not for profit or is a "qualified referral service," which means that it has been approved by the appropriate regulatory authority. **Answer (A) is incorrect** because regulatory approval is not necessary if the service is non-profit, as it is here. **Answer (C) is incorrect** because Antonio is allowed to pay the usual charges of such a non-profit service. Answer (B) is, therefore, correct. **Answer (D) is wrong** because it is not enough that Antonio does not own or operate the service, although those would be relevant factors if he tried to obtain regulatory approval for a referral service. See Comment 6 to Rule 7.2. If, for example, the service was for profit and not "qualified," payments to the service would be improper even if Antonio did not own or operate it. Answer (B) is correct.

105. **The correct answer is (D).** Mary Jane is planning to engage in telephonic solicitation for employment as a lawyer for pecuniary gain. That is improper unless an exception applies, and the only one that applies is that the prospective client is a lawyer. The rules assume that Patrick can protect himself against solicitation by a trained advocate because of his legal training. **Answer (A) is incorrect** because an exception applies to solicitation for pecuniary gain when the target is a lawyer. **Answer (B) is incorrect** because the two stated exceptions to the anti-solicitation rule are not the only ones. Another one, that the prospective client is a lawyer, applies here. **Answer (C) is incorrect** because a lawyer's solicitation will be permitted if it is to a close family member, not to someone unknown to the lawyer but married to a close family member. The reason for the exception for a close family member is that the rules assume a lawyer would not take advantage of such a person. That assumption is slightly less justifiable when the connection is merely by marriage to a close family

member. Answer (D) is correct.

106.   **The correct answer is (C).** Under Rule 7.1, lawyers are permitted to advertise their services as long as the communication is not false or misleading. **Answer (A) is wrong** because it is not enough for the statement to be literally true. If it is misleading, the communication violates Rule 7.1. This statement by itself would be misleading because it omits a crucial fact: that the lawyer paid to be on the list. Without that additional information, the statement would lead a reasonable person to conclude that some objective body had found William to be among the best lawyers. Answer (C) is, therefore, correct. See Comments 1 and 2 to Rule 7.1. **Answer (B) is incorrect** because the lawyer's constitutional right to advertise does not include the right to make false or misleading statements. **Answer (D) is incorrect** because lawyers are permitted to compare their services if the comparison can be substantiated. See Comment 3 to Rule 7.1. Answer (C) is correct.

107.   **The correct answer is (D).** Under Rule 8.4(e), lawyers are not permitted to state or imply an ability to achieve results by means that violate the rules of conduct or other law. This advertisement, with one more ace than a deck of cards allows, and with a phone number that includes the word "cheater," does exactly that. **Answer (A) is wrong** because this is not a matter generally of taste. It is a question of a lawyer specifically advertising the ability to help clients by cheating. **Answer (B) is incorrect** because the danger is not client perception but rather the encouragement of illegal conduct and damage to public perception about the profession and the system. Truthfully stating that you cheat the system is still a violation. **Answer (C) is incorrect** because there is no such general standard for advertising. This ad runs afoul of a specific prohibition, and the underlying concern is in part disrepute for the profession and the legal system, but the answer as stated is too general. Answer (D) is correct.

108.   Sonny has two problems. Under Rule 7.1, he may not advertise in any way that is false and misleading. The statement that you will "save money" by hiring him is a comparison of the cost of his services with the competition. Similarly, to say "Guest is the best" is a comparison of the quality of his services with the services of other lawyers. The risk is that these statements may be construed to have been presented with sufficient specificity as to cause a reasonable person to believe that they can be substantiated. If the statements do give rise to that reasonable belief, and they cannot be substantiated, they are misleading under Rule 7.1. See Comment 3 to Rule 7.1.

109.   Hattie's problem is that using the headlines, even if they are truthful, may create an unjustified expectation in the minds of potential clients that Hattie can secure similar results for them. That unjustified expectation would mean that the advertisement would be misleading under Rule 7.1. See Comment 3 to Rule 7.1. If Hattie wants to use the headlines, she will need to include a disclaimer, for example, that she cannot necessarily obtain results like the results depicted or that all cases must be evaluated on their own merits.

110.   Rita needs to be particularly careful about in-person solicitation of clients. Although nothing in the Rules of Professional Conduct forbids a lawyer from educating the public about legal issues, this plan will put Rita face-to-face with people she hopes will become clients. Under Rule 7.3, she may not solicit employment from them unless they are lawyers or Rita has a previous professional, family, or close personal relationship with them. Rule 7.3(a). Although

Rita may certainly respond to requests for assistance from attendees who initiate contact with her, she may not initiate the relationship by soliciting employment.

111.   **The correct answer is (B).** It is apparent to Raymond that Marvin's abuse of alcohol is causing a mental condition that materially impairs Marvin's ability to represent his clients. Therefore, Raymond knows that Marvin has an obligation to withdraw from those representations under Rule 1.16(a)(2). Marvin's failure to do so is a violation of the Rules that raises a substantial question as to his fitness, which triggers the mandatory reporting requirement of Rule 8.3. See ABA Formal Op. 03-431. **Answer (A) is incorrect** because reporting under these circumstances is required rather than optional. **Answer (C) is incorrect** because Marvin is violating a rule, namely Rule 1.16(a)(2). **Answer (D) is incorrect** because, although a lawyer has the option to report a fellow lawyer to a lawyers assistance program, such a report does not relieve a lawyer of any obligation that otherwise exists to report that fellow lawyer to the appropriate professional authority. See ABA Formal Op. 03-431.

112.   **The correct answer is (D).** Lawyers have an obligation to report violations of the rules of conduct by other lawyers if those violations reflect adversely on the other lawyer's honesty, trustworthiness, or fitness as a lawyer in other respects. Rule 8.3(a). **Answer (A) is wrong** because embezzlement is a crime of dishonesty, and under Rule 8.4(b) it is misconduct for a lawyer to commit a crime that reflects upon his or her honesty, trustworthiness, or fitness. It does not matter that neither April nor the Dean is a practicing lawyer. See ABA Formal Op. 04-433. The obligation to report still exists, so **Answers (B) and (C) are incorrect.** Only (D) accurately states that April must report the Dean for his criminal act.

113.   **The correct answer is (D).** At first glance, Bryan has a reporting obligation under Rule 8.3 because Cassandra has violated Rule 3.4(a) in a way that reflects adversely on her honesty, trustworthiness, and fitness as a lawyer. However, the obligation to report does not trump the lawyer's duty of confidentiality. See Comment 2 to Rule 1.6. Here, Bryan could report with the informed consent of his client to disclose to the bar information relating to the representation, but Bryan would have to advise his client that doing so is not in the client's best interest because of the danger to the settlement talks. **Answer (A) is incorrect** because the mandate to report does not apply when the information is confidential and the lawyer does not have client consent to reveal it. **Answer (B) is incorrect** because the reporting obligation is mandatory if there is no confidentiality problem and forbidden if there is. **Answer (C) is incorrect** because it is incomplete. Bryan has a confidentiality problem, but it could be overcome with consent. Answer (D) is correct.

114.   **The correct answer is (A).** Under Rule 4.1(A)(8) of the Model Code of Judicial Conduct, Kayla was not permitted to personally solicit campaign contributions. Her violation of that rule was also a violation of Model Rule of Professional Conduct 8.2, which requires candidates for judicial office to comply with applicable provisions of the Code of Judicial Conduct. **Answers (B) and (C) are incorrect** because they are incomplete. She violated both the Code and the Rules. **Answer (D) is incorrect** because Kayla did violate rules of

conduct. Answer (A) is correct.

115. **The correct answer is (C).** Rule 8.4 defines misconduct. Under Rule 8.4(a), it is misconduct to attempt to violate the Rules of Professional Conduct. Here, Adam attempted an act that, if he had succeeded, would have been to unlawfully destroy items of potential evidentiary value, in violation of Rule 3.4(a). Therefore, he committed misconduct under Rule 8.4(a). **Answer (A) is incorrect** because the attempt to violate a rule is misconduct, whether he succeeds or not. **Answer (B) is incorrect** because it is not necessary that Adam commit a crime to be guilty of misconduct. Commission of certain crimes is misconduct, but that is not the only type of misconduct. **Answer (D) is incorrect** because, although the commission of such a criminal act is misconduct under Rule 8.4(b), the attempt to commit such a criminal act is not misconduct under that Rule. Answer (C) is correct.

116. **The correct answer is (A).** Under Rule 8.5(a), a lawyer is subject to discipline in the state where he or she is admitted regardless of where the conduct occurs, and a lawyer is subject to discipline in a state where the lawyer provides legal services. A lawyer may be responsible to more than one disciplinary authority for the same conduct. **Answers (D) and (B) are incorrect** because they limit the disciplinary authority of one state or the other. **Answer (C) is incorrect.** It correctly states one factor that helps to determine which state's rules will apply as a matter of choice of law, but that factor is not relevant to the question of which state or states may discipline a lawyer for misconduct. Because both states may do so, Answer (A) is correct.

117. **The correct answer is (A).** The general rule on criminal conduct is Rule 8.4(b), which defines misconduct to include criminal acts that reflect adversely on the lawyer's honesty, truthfulness, or fitness as a lawyer in other respects. Criminal violations that do not show that the lawyer lacks some character trait necessary for law practice do not count as misconduct. See Comment 2 to Rule 8.4. A minor traffic ticket is in this category. **Answer (B) is incorrect** because it is irrelevant that Sean got his ticket while doing something for a client. The offense still does not demonstrate dishonesty, lack of trustworthiness, or unfitness in some other respect. **Answer (C) is incorrect** because there are circumstances under which a lawyer's traffic offenses might constitute misconduct. For example, repeated offenses for driving under the influence could reflect on the lawyer's fitness. **Answer (D) is incorrect** because it is not automatically misconduct when a lawyer shows disrespect for the law. Repeated violations of the law can constitute misconduct, but one traffic ticket, even if it arose from disrespect for the speed limit, would not mean that the lawyer was unfit and should be disciplined. Answer (A) is correct.

118. ABA Formal Opinion 03-429 discusses the obligations of lawyers in a firm when someone in the firm is impaired, and the opinion also discusses the lawyer's obligations when the impaired lawyer leaves. Here, Ellen's partner is impaired and has left the firm with some of her clients. According to the opinion, the firm has no obligation to warn those former clients about the impairment. The firm should avoid any action that would appear to be an endorsement of the departing lawyer, but there is no duty to warn someone who is no longer your client. See Rule 1.4 (detailing duties of communication with clients).

119. Clara has information that the opposing lawyer has assisted in a fraud in violation of Rule 1.2(a). The other lawyer also committed misconduct under Rule 8.4(c). Clara therefore has an obligation, subject to the client's permission to reveal confidential information, to report

the fraud to the bar because the violations reflect adversely on the other lawyer's honesty, trustworthiness, or fitness as a lawyer. A threat to do that implies that she will refrain from doing so if the lawyer capitulates during the negotiation. Indeed, that would seem to be the only purpose of the threat. Yet Clara has a duty to report. ABA Formal Opinion 94-383 holds that a lawyer in Clara's situation may not use a threat to comply with her mandatory reporting duty as a ploy in a negotiation.

120. Under Rule 8.2(a), Richard may not make any statement he knows to be false or with reckless disregard of its falsity about the qualifications or integrity of his rival. Now that Edward is a candidate for appointment to judicial office, Richard like all other members of the bar must not say things that unfairly undermine public confidence in the administration of justice. See Comment 1 to Rule 8.2.

121.   **The correct answer is (C).** Under Rule 3.11(B)(1), the judge may serve as a manager of a business closely held by the judge or members of the judge's family, subject to certain conditions, one of which is that doing so will not interfere with the proper performance of judicial duties. **Answer (A) is incorrect** because a family business is an exception to the general rule that a sitting judge shall not serve as an officer, director, manager, general partner, advisor, or employee of any business entity. Rule 3.11(B). **Answer (B) is incorrect** because the location of the business does not cure all the potential problems. While its location probably means that the judge's involvement is unlikely to lead to frequent disqualification and is unlikely to involve the judge in frequent transactions or continuing business relationships with lawyers or others likely to come before his court (see Rule 3.11(C)(2) and (3)), it still could take too much of the judge's time. **Answer (D) is incorrect** because it is not enough that the business is owned by the judge's family. The judge's participation is still constrained by the provisions of Rule 3.11(C), which includes the proviso that the involvement must not interfere with the proper performance of judicial duties. Answer (C) is correct.

122.   **The correct answer is (C).** Rule 2.2 requires the judge to uphold and apply the law, and her duty here is to apply it without regard to her personal feelings. See Comment 2 to Rule 2.2. **Answers (A) and (D) are incorrect** because the judge does not have the option, much less the duty, to recuse herself just because she disapproves of the law. To the contrary, she has the duty to sit unless there is a basis for disqualification, which there is not. See Rule 2.7 (duty to sit) and Rule 2.11 (disqualification). It is given in the question that the judge's impartiality could not reasonably be questioned. **Answer (B) is incorrect** because the judge is not free to fashion "substantial justice." The judge must follow the law. Answer (C) is correct.

123.   **The correct answer is (A).** Under Rule 2.3, judges are prohibited from manifesting bias or prejudice based upon a number of factors, including sexual orientation. **Answer (B) is therefore incorrect.** The parties' sexual orientations are irrelevant to their business dispute, and therefore references to these characteristics are manifestations of bias or prejudice. See Comment 2 to Rule 2.3. It does not matter if sexual orientation is part of the evidence. What matters is whether sexual orientation is relevant to an issue in the proceeding, and it is difficult to see how it could be in a business dispute. **Answers (C) and (D), therefore, are incorrect.** Answer (A) is correct.

124.   **The correct answer is (A).** Under Rule 2.6, judges may encourage parties to settle matters as long as the judge is not coercive. Comment 2 describes the factors the judge should consider as the judge tries to determine whether the judge's involvement in any particular negotiation would be coercive, but there is no general ban on judicial involvement in negotiations. **Answers (B) and (C) are incorrect** because judges are not banned from negotiations in bench cases or criminal cases, although these are factors for the judge to

consider under Comment 2 to Rule 2.6. **Answer (D) is incorrect** because there is no prohibition of judicial involvement in negotiations. Answer (A) is correct.

125.   **The correct answer is (B).** Under Rule 2.8, the judge is permitted to meet with the jurors after trial but must be careful not to commend or criticize the verdict (Rule 2.8(C)) or discuss the merits of the case (Comment 3 to Rule 2.8). **Answer (A) is incorrect** because it is incomplete. It is not enough to refrain from comment about the verdict. The judge must also steer clear of discussion the merits of the case otherwise. **Answer (C) is incorrect** because the parties have no right to attend. The trial is over, and the judge may choose to meet with the jurors without the lawyers present. **Answer (D) is incorrect** because under the right conditions the judge is permitted to meet with jurors after the trial. Answer (B) is correct.

126.   **The correct answer is (B).** Under Rule 2.9(A)(2), the judge was permitted to obtain written advice from a disinterested expert on the law, but was required to give advance written notice to the parties. Here, the parties did not receive advance notice, and the advice was not in writing, both of which make it difficult for the losing party to counter whatever advice the retired judge gave. **Answer (A) is incorrect** because, under the right conditions, judges are permitted to receive expert advice on the law from a disinterested expert. **Answer (C) is incorrect** because, although the judge is entitled to seek disinterested advice, there are procedural safeguards in place (the advice must be in writing, with advance notice to the parties) to make sure the parties can dispute the advice. **Answer (D) is incorrect** because telling the parties about the advice orally, after it has been given, is not a sufficient opportunity for the parties to respond to the advice. Answer (B) is correct.

127.   **The correct answer is (D).** Under Rule 2.10(A), judges are not permitted to make any public statement that might reasonably be expected to affect the outcome or impair the fairness of a proceeding in any court. **Answer (A) is incorrect** because the prohibition applies to matters pending in any court and not just his. **Answer (C) is incorrect** because the judge is required by Rule 2.10(C) to require his staff to refrain from making statements that the judge cannot make himself. If the statements at the press conference might reasonably be expected to affect the outcome or impair the fairness of a proceeding, then having the clerk make them is still a violation of Rule 2.10. **Answer (B) is incorrect** because the judge is a party to the mandamus proceeding only in an official (rather than a personal) capacity. See Comment 3 to Rule 2.10. Answer (D) is correct.

128.   **The correct answer is (A).** Under Rule 2.11(A), judges must disqualify themselves whenever their impartiality might reasonably be questioned. In addition to that general standard, the rule provides a list of circumstances in which it is conclusively presumed that the standard is met. Among those circumstances is the material witness who is too close to the judge. How close is too close? Rule 2.11(A)(2) establishes those boundaries. It includes the judge's domestic partner. It also includes anyone within the third degree of relationship to the judge's domestic partner, so the sister would be too close. The Rule also, however, extends the range of the automatic disqualification to the spouse of "such a person," meaning the spouse of someone within the third degree of relationship to the judge or the judge's domestic partner. Since the witness is the spouse of someone within the third degree of relationship to the judge's domestic partner, disqualification is automatic. **Answer (B) is incorrect** because not everyone related to the domestic partner would cause automatic disqualification. Anyone not within the third degree of relationship — for example, a cousin — would be outside that zone. **Answer (C) is incorrect** because under the rule the

relationship is not too remote. **Answer (D) is incorrect** because the presumption is conclusive that the judge's impartiality might reasonably be questioned when a person this close is a material witness. The judge's judgment about that is irrelevant. Answer (A) is correct.

129.   **The correct answer is (A).** This judge would normally be disqualified from acting as a judge in this matter because a person within the third degree of relationship has more than a de minimis interest that could be substantially affected by the proceeding. See Rule 2.11(A)(2)(c). However, the rule of necessity will override this conflict because there are no other judges available to hear the matter. The judge must rule, make a record of his conflict, and make reasonable efforts to transfer the case to another judge as soon as practicable. Comment 3 to Rule 2.11. **Answer (D) is incorrect** because the grandson's interest in the corporation that owns the property that is to be foreclosed on is more than a de minimis interest. The foreclosure will affect the value of the grandson's stock (the office building is the corporation's only asset), and that is more than a de minimis interest. **Answer (B) is incorrect** because the judge must rule. It is not merely an option. **Answer (C) is incorrect** because the necessity of the circumstances dictates that the judge rule despite the application. Answer (A) accurately describes the judge's responsibilities.

130.   **The correct answer is (C).** Under Rule 2.14, the judge is required to take appropriate action to deal with a lawyer like Leo, whose performance apparently has been impaired by a physical condition. The Model Rules of Judicial Conduct do not restrictively define what "appropriate action" is, but it must be intended to and reasonably likely to help the lawyer address the problem and prevent harm to the system. In this case, it might be enough to speak to Leo and make sure he sees a neurologist to be tested for any signs of Alzheimer's or other senile dementia. **Answer (A) is incorrect** because the judge is required to take action. Doing so is not merely an option. **Answer (B) is incorrect** because referral to a lawyers assistance program is one of many options for the judge in this case. It is not the only one. See Comment 1 to Rule 2.14. **Answer (D) is incorrect** because the judge has not observed a violation of the Rules of Professional Conduct. Under Rule 2.15, the judge must report a lawyer to the disciplinary authorities only when the judge knows that the lawyer has committed a violation of the Rules of Professional Conduct that raises a substantial question as to that lawyer's honesty, trustworthiness, or fitness as a lawyer in other respects. Answer (C) is correct.

131.   **The correct answer is (C).** Under Rule 3.1, judges are permitted to engage in extrajudicial activities, subject to some restrictions. One of those restrictions is that the judge must not do anything that would appear to a reasonable person to undermine the judge's independence, integrity, or impartiality. Comment 3 to Rule 3.1 states that a racist joke is an example of an extrajudicial activity that would do so. **Answer (A) is incorrect** because even a joke can affect a reasonable person's perception of the judge's impartiality. Such a reasonable person could readily wonder whether someone who truly has no racial prejudices would tell such jokes. **Answer (B) is incorrect** because the code regulates extrajudicial conduct as well as judicial conduct, and the making of a racist joke is one example of extrajudicial conduct that violates the code. **Answer (D) is incorrect** because judges are encouraged to participate in civic activities, even those unrelated to the law, as long as certain conditions are met. Participation in the "Endzone Club" is not, in and of itself, a violation of the Code. Answer (C) is correct.

132. **The correct answer is (D).** Under Rule 3.2, judges are permitted under limited circumstances to appear voluntarily at a public hearing of a governmental body. Answer (D) is correct because one of those circumstances is a pro se appearance in a matter that involves the judge's legal interests. Rule 3.2(C); see also Comment 3 to Rule 3.2. **Answer (B) is incorrect** because, although under Rule 3.2(A) judges may voluntarily appear before governmental bodies on matters concerning the law, this appearance is not about the law generally but about a particular matter. Furthermore, that general permission is not needed when the judge's appearance is specifically permitted by Rule 3.2(C). **Answer (C) is incorrect** because the judge is permitted to appear, although he must be careful not to refer to his judicial office or use the prestige of his office. Comment 3 to Rule 3.2. **Answer (A) is incorrect** because this is one of the few circumstances in which a judge may appear voluntarily. Answer (D) is correct.

133. **The correct answer is (A).** Under Rule 3.6(B), the judge was prohibited from using the facilities of an organization that he knew practiced invidious discrimination. To choose that club for his daughter's reception could be seen by a reasonable person to be an endorsement of the club's discriminatory policies. **Answer (B) is incorrect** because the judge could attend an isolated event at a place like the club. The problem here is that he personally chose to use the facilities for this event. He was not merely a guest. **Answer (C) is incorrect** because membership is not the only way to violate the code when a club that practices invidious discrimination is involved. Use of the facilities of such an organization is also a violation. **Answer (D) is incorrect** because even an isolated use, as opposed to isolated attendance, could be seen as an endorsement of the club's policies and is therefore prohibited. Answer (A) is correct.

134. **The correct answer is (B).** Rule 3.7 governs judges' participation in educational, religious, charitable, fraternal, or civic organizations. Under Rule 3.7(A)(3), the judge would be permitted to solicit membership for the Inn, even though it requires payment of dues, because the Inn is devoted to the administration of justice. Answer (B), therefore, is correct. **Answer (A) is incorrect** because the limitations listed apply to solicitation of contributions to organizations rather than solicitations of membership. See Rule 3.7(A)(2). **Answer (C) is incorrect** because Rule 3.7(A)(3) explicitly permits this activity, even though it may seem coercive to some members of the bar. **Answer (D) is incorrect** because payment of dues for membership in an organization devoted to the administration of justice is treated differently from general contributions to organizations. Compare Rule 3.7(A)(2) and Rule 3.7(A)(3). Answer (B) is correct.

135. **The correct answer is (D).** Under Rule 3.10, the judge is prohibited from representing anyone, including a family member, in any forum. This is part of the general prohibition on judges practicing law, but the rule specifically bans any representation of anyone in court. **Answer (A) is incorrect** because judges may not appear in court as a lawyer, even for a family member. **Answer (B) is incorrect** because there is no "emergency" exception to the general rule that judges may not appear in any forum as the lawyer for any client. **Answer (C) is incorrect** because Rule 3.10 specifically bans the representation of a client in court, although Comment 1 does also mention that generally judges may not use the prestige of their office to advance personal interests or the interests of family members. Answer (D) is correct.

136. **The correct answer is (D).** Judges are permitted to engage in extrajudicial activities such

as writing, subject to certain exceptions. One of the exceptions is that a judge shall not participate in extrajudicial activities that interfere with the proper performance of judicial activities. Rule 3.1(A). **Answers (A) and (B) are incorrect** because they state conditions that allow for compensation under Rule 3.12 for extrajudicial activities, but only for such activities that are permitted by the Code. Anything that interferes with the judge's proper performance of judicial duties is not permitted by the Code. **Answer (C) is incorrect** because writing is a permitted extrajudicial activity, and there is no requirement that such writing concern the law. Answer (D) is correct.

137. **The correct answer is (C).** Under Rule 3.13(B)(4), judges may accept special pricing and discounts only if the terms are available to similarly situated persons who are not judges. The bank officer made it clear that this was a "judge discount" and therefore not available to others. **Answers (A) and (B) are incorrect** because the prohibition on accepting special discounts is unrelated to whether the person or entity giving the discount is currently or frequently a litigant. The underlying problem is that acceptance of special favors will appear to a reasonable person to undermine the judge's integrity. **Answer (D) is incorrect** because it is overbroad. Judges can accept commercial discounts as long as they are available to similarly situated persons who are not judges and as long as they do not otherwise create in the mind of a reasonable person the appearance that the judge's independence, impartiality, or integrity has been undermined. Answer (C) is correct.

138. **The correct answer is (A).** Rule 3.14 governs reimbursement of expenses. A number of things must be true before a judge can accept reimbursement of expenses. **Answer (D) is incorrect** because it is not enough that the judge is being reimbursed for participating in an extrajudicial activity permitted by the Code. That requirement, which comes from Rule 3.14(A), is subject to the caveat that reimbursement must not be prohibited by, among other things, Rule 3.13(A). That Rule prohibits a judge from accepting anything of value if acceptance would appear to a reasonable person to undermine the judge's independence, integrity, or impartiality. For a judge sitting in a court that handles cases involving drugs to accept benefits from a trade association that represents drug companies would do so. See Comment 3 to Rule 3.14. Answer (A), therefore, is correct. **Answer (B) is incorrect** because the judge may not accept the reimbursement even if it is only for his actual costs reasonably incurred, although that is an additional requirement in addition to those just described. See Rule 3.14(B). **Answer (C) is incorrect** for the same reason. The judge must report the payment of expenses that the judge properly accepts, but reimbursement of these expenses would violate Rule 3.13(A). Answer (A) is correct.

139. **The correct answer is (B).** Judges may act as fiduciaries only under the conditions set forth in Rule 3.8. One such condition is that the judge would be acting for a member of the judge's family. Here, she would be acting for her deceased husband's parents, but 'member of the judge's family" is defined in the Terminology section of the Code to include any person with whom the judge maintains a close familial relationship. Judge Reeves has such a relationship with the beneficiaries of these trusts and therefore can act as trustee, given the other circumstances recited in the question. **Answer (A) is incorrect** because it is overbroad. Even if service as trustee would not interfere with the proper performance of judicial duties, judges may not act as trustees except for members of the judge's family. **Answer (C) is incorrect** because a close familial relationship is enough to permit the judge to act as trustee. The judge need not actually be related to the beneficiaries. **Answer (D) is incorrect**

because under the right circumstances, judges are allowed to act as fiduciaries. Answer (B) is correct.

140.   **The correct answer is (C).** The judge's obligation under Rule 2.2 is to perform all duties of judicial office fairly and impartially. Comment 4 to Rule 2.2 makes it clear that a judge does not violate this rule if the judge makes reasonable accommodations to ensure that pro se litigants have the opportunity to have their matters fairly heard. Answer (C), therefore, is correct. **Answer (A) is incorrect** because the judge has this discretion. **Answer (B) is incorrect** because there is no general right to appointed counsel in civil matters. **Answer (D) is incorrect** because the judge is permitted to make reasonable accommodations, but nothing in the Code of Judicial Conduct requires the judge to do so. Answer (C) is correct.

141.   **The correct answer is (A).** A presentencing report would not be part of the court record and therefore is nonpublic information. A judge is generally not permitted to use nonpublic information, but the judge may use such information to warn court personnel of danger. Comment 2 to Rule 3.5. **Answer (B) is not correct** because the general rule is that judges may not use nonpublic information for any purpose other than discharge of the judge's judicial duties. **Answer (C) is incorrect** because the general prohibition on the use of nonpublic information does not prevent the judge from using it to warn judicial officers of danger. **Answer (D) is incorrect** because the presentencing report is not confidential. It is nonpublic, which restricts the judge's use of it, but there are no confidentiality obligations that would prevent the judge from warning the deputy. Answer (A) is correct.

142.   **The correct answer is (C).** Rule 2.9(B) governs the receipt of inadvertent ex parte communications. The judge is required to notify the parties of the substance of the communication and provide them with an opportunity to respond. Answer (C), therefore, is correct. **Answer (A) is incorrect** because the opposing party is entitled to know that an ex parte communication has occurred and is entitled to know what it is. **Answer (B) is incorrect** because the parties need to know not just the fact of the ex parte communication but also its content. **Answer (D) is incorrect** because it is impossible to "unring the bell." The judge has received the communication and now the parties must be notified. Answer (C) is correct.

143.   **The correct answer is (B).** Judge Laird has a personal prejudice concerning a party and thus must disqualify himself under Rule 2.11(A)(1). **Answer (A) is incorrect** because no motion to disqualify is required. See Comment 2 to Rule 2.11. **Answer (C) is incorrect** because parties may not consent to a judge remaining on a case when the basis for disqualification is personal prejudice against a party. Rule 2.11(C). **Answer (D) is incorrect** because the recusal is a duty rather than an option. Answer (B) is correct.

144.   **The correct answer is (B).** Judges generally are not to accept appointments to governmental commissions except for commissions, like this one, that concern the law. Rule 3.4. Answer (B), therefore, is correct. **Answer (A) is incorrect** because there is not a blanket prohibition on judges serving on government commissions. In fact, judges are expressly permitted to do so on commissions that deal with the law. **Answer (C) is incorrect** because it is too broad. Even if an appointment to a government commission would not interfere with the proper performance of judicial duties, a judge may not accept such an appointment unless it concerns the law, the legal system, or the administration of justice. **Answer (D) is incorrect** because there is no requirement that a judge have special expertise to accept an

appointment to a government commission that concerns the law, the legal system, or the administration of justice. Answer (B) is correct.

145. **The correct answer is (A).** Participation in the activities of religious organizations is governed by Rule 3.7. **Answer (D) is incorrect** because attendance at an event, even if it involves fund-raising, is not a violation. See Comment 3 to Rule 3.7. **Answers (B) and (C) are incorrect** because service as an usher is deemed not to be solicitation and not to be coercive or abusive. Id. Answer (A) is correct because the risks of judicial participation in fund-raising activities are not deemed by the Code to exist under these circumstances.

146. **The correct answer is (A).** The judge is investigating facts. He has evidence that the defendant performed some procedure and is investigating what it was. Under Rule 2.9(C), the judge is not permitted to undertake any independent investigation of the facts. Here, the judge might read the results of his internet search and assume that the defendant did something that the defendant did not do. If the judge needs to know more, he should ask the parties or ask the experts questions in open court. **Answer (B) is incorrect** because the judge is not permitted to do this kind of investigation. **Answers (C) and (D) are incorrect** because they presume that the judge's investigation is permissible with pre- or post-investigation notice to the parties. The judge simply is not allowed to investigate facts. Answer (A) is the correct answer.

147. **The correct answer is (D).** Under Rule 2.10(A), judges are generally prohibited from making any public statements that might substantially interfere with the fairness of a trial or hearing. Subject to this prohibition, a judge is permitted to respond to allegations of misconduct. Rule 2.10(E). Answer (D), therefore, is correct. **Answer (B) is incorrect** because the judge has the limited right to respond, even when the trial is ongoing. **Answer (C) is incorrect** because even truthful responses could undermine the fairness of the trial, and the judge is not permitted to do that. **Answer (A) is incorrect** because, although Rule 2.10(E) permits the judge to respond through a third party, the third party still must limit his or her remarks in order to minimize the danger of interfering with a fair trial. Answer (D) is correct.

148. **The correct answer is (C).** Under Rule 2.11(A)(5), the judge must be disqualified because she has made a public statement as a judicial candidate that commits or appears to commit her to decide this case in a particular way. **Answer (A) is incorrect** because it is not the source of the judge's opinion but rather her expression of it as a commitment that gives rise to disqualification. **Answer (B) is incorrect** because Rule 2.11 lists this circumstance as one in which her impartiality might reasonably be questioned. It is not up to the judge to decide whether this specifically listed circumstance meets that general criterion. **Answer (D) is incorrect** because the judge has no discretion about disqualifying herself once the commitment has been made, or once it appears that the commitment has been made. Answer (C) is correct.

149. **The correct answer is (C).** Rule 3.6 prohibits judges from being members of organizations that practice invidious discrimination on the basis of race, sex, gender, religion, national origin, ethnicity, or sexual orientation. Comment 4 to the Rule, however, makes it clear that a judge does not violate the rule by being a member of a religious organization as part of the judge's lawful exercise of freedom of religion. Mr. Meyer, therefore, could remain as a member of his church and still be in compliance with the Code of Judicial Conduct. **Answer**

(A) is incorrect because the judge need not resign. **Answer (B) is incorrect** because Rule 3.6 does generally prohibit membership in organizations that practice invidious discrimination based upon sexual orientation. **Answer (D) is incorrect** because Mr. Meyer need not resign at all. Furthermore, if he did have the obligation to resign, he would be obliged under Rule 3.6 to do so immediately. Comment 3 to Rule 3.6. Answer (C) is correct.

150.   **The correct answer is (A).** Rule 3.7 regulates judges' participation in educational, religious, charitable, fraternal, and civic organizations and activities. Under Rule 3.7(A)(2), a judge's ability to solicit contributions for such an entity is severely circumscribed because of the risk of coercion. However, as Comment 4 makes clear, it is not a violation of this rule to allow the judge's name and title to be used on letterhead for a solicitation letter as long as comparable designations are used for others. **Answer (B) is incorrect** because judges are generally not permitted to solicit contributions to such organizations except from members of the judge's family or other judges over whom the judge does not exercise supervisory or appellate authority. Rule 3.7(A)(2). This letter is a general solicitation. **Answer (C) is incorrect** because, as long as comparable designations are used for others on the letterhead, the letter could not reasonably be seen as an attempt to trade on judicial prestige or coerce a gift. **Answer (D) is incorrect** because it is overbroad. To the limited extent described in the question, judges may participate in fund-raising. Answer (A) is correct.

151.   Judge Owens has a number of choices. If the judge knew that the lawyer had destroyed evidence, the judge would have no choice under Rule 2.15(B) except to report the lawyer to the appropriate authority. Because the judge merely has a reasonable belief but does not know that the lawyer has done so, his obligation under Rule 2.15(D) is to take "appropriate action." That action may be to report the lawyer to the appropriate authority, but it could also include lesser measure such as speaking to the lawyer about it directly or communicating with the lawyer's supervisor. See Comment 2 to Rule 2.15.

152.   Judge Clarke violated Rule 2.11(B), which requires him to stay informed about his personal and fiduciary economic interests. The interest of the church in the property is an economic interest that the judge should have been aware of. The judge did not violate Rule 2.11 by not recusing himself from the underlying case because disqualification requires that the judge know the reason why he is disqualified. Judge Clarke's violation was in not staying informed.

153.   The judge violated Rule 3.5, which forbids the judge to release nonpublic information (defined in the Terminology section of the Code to include grand jury proceedings) for any purpose unrelated to the judge's judicial duties. It is irrelevant that the judge acted in the public interest rather than from a selfish motive. The judge revealed nonpublic information for a political purpose, and that was outside the performance of the judge's judicial duties.

154.   The Model Code of Judicial Conduct does not specifically address how candidates should respond to campaign questionnaires, but the usual problem is the responses would constitute pledges, promises, or commitments to decide issues in a certain way, and that is not permitted campaign speech. Rule 4.1(A)(13). However, it does not violate the Code of Judicial Conduct to make promises about judicial administration or organization, such as promises to dispose of a backlog of cases or start court on time. The candidate may respond freely to this questionnaire.

155.   The judge is not bound to recuse himself under any of the specific sets of circumstances in

Rule 2.11. The ex-wife is not related to him, and he does not have a personal bias or prejudice about her. Nevertheless, it is still possible that the judge would have to recuse himself if his impartiality might reasonably be questioned. If, for example, his divorce was high profile and bitter, then others may reasonably question his ability to be impartial even though he subjectively knows that he is not bitter.

156. The judge may accept reimbursement of her expenses as long as they are reasonable and necessary and are not prohibited by Rule 3.1 or 3.13(A). Rule 3.14(A). The expenses are incurred in connection with a permitted extrajudicial activity, and it is difficult to imagine how reimbursement by the state bar would appear to undermine the judge's independence, integrity, or impartiality (and thereby violate Rule 3.13(A)). Such reimbursement also would not appear to violate any of the general rules on extrajudicial activities in Rule 3.1. The judge's husband's expenses may be reimbursed if doing so is "appropriate to the occasion." Rule 3.14(B).

157. Graham may not use the endorsement. Rule 4.1(A)(7) forbids candidates for judicial office from seeking, accepting, or using endorsements from political organizations. No matter how helpful it would be, the endorsement from the state Democratic Party would be an endorsement from a political organization, and the candidate may not use it.

158. Judge Bridges has learned that the other judge violated the Code of Judicial Conduct. Rule 2.4(B) forbids judges to permit personal or political interests to influence the judge's conduct. Furthermore, this is a violation of the Code that reflects adversely on the other judge's fitness as a judge. Judge Bridges now has the obligation under Rule 2.15(A) to report her fellow judge to the appropriate disciplinary authority.

159. The judge can keep the trophy without reporting it. Rule 3.13 governs the acceptance and reporting of gifts, loans, bequests, and other things of value. Under Rule 3.13(B)(1), the judge may accept without publicly reporting items such as trophies that have little intrinsic value, as long as acceptance would not appear to a reasonable person to undermine the judge's independence, integrity, or impartiality. Here, a trophy from law students, especially first-year students who are a long way from appearing in his courtroom, would not give such an appearance, and therefore the judge may keep the trophy without bothering to report it.

160. Judge Parsons need not insist on rejection of the television, and he need not report its receipt. Under Rule 3.13(B)(8), the judge may accept without reporting the incidental benefits of gifts, awards, or benefits associated with the business of the judge's spouse. There is nothing in these circumstances to indicate that the broker is giving the award in order to benefit the judge and circumvent the usual rules on giving gifts to judges. See Comment 4 to Rule 3.13. The judge has no obligation to do anything about the television.

PRACTICE FINAL EXAM: ANSWERS

161. **The correct answer is (C).** Biff's statement is information relating to Melinda's representation of him. Therefore, Melinda is obliged to keep it confidential unless there is an exception. Although there is an exception when the attorney reasonably believes that disclosure is necessary to prevent reasonably certain death or substantial bodily harm, here the lawyer does not believe disclosure is necessary. Therefore, the exception does not apply and the lawyer is bound to keep the information confidential. **Answer (A) is incorrect** because the exception that would allow Melinda the option to reveal does not apply. **Answer (B) is incorrect** because the exception does not apply and, furthermore, because disclosure would be optional rather than mandatory even if it did apply. **Answer (D) is incorrect** because Melinda must withdraw under only three circumstances: continuing the representation would cause her to violate the Rules of Professional Conduct, her mental or physical condition materially impairs her ability to represent the client, or she is discharged. None of these conditions are present. Answer (C) is the correct answer.

162. **The correct answer is (C).** There is a risk of a conflict of interest between the insurance company and the policyholder, but usually the interests of the two are aligned. As long as the clients (policyholders) are informed that their lawyer works for the insurance company, and as long as the lawyer exercises independent judgment on behalf of the client, the client is protected and the arrangement is permitted. See ABA Formal Op. 03-340. **Answer (A) is wrong** because the arrangement is permitted under the right conditions. **Answer (B) is wrong** because, although staff counsel can practice in a law firm setting and under a trade name, there is no requirement that they do so. Id. **Answer (D) is wrong** even though the interests of the company and the policyholder are more aligned in a full coverage case. The permissibility of the arrangement, however, is not dependent upon this circumstance. Id. Answer (C) is correct.

163. **The correct answer is (D).** Sam is an attorney for an entity. Rule 1.13(a). He has gathered confidential information about clear violations of the law and reasonably believes that the violations are reasonably certain to cause substantial injury to the organization. He further reasonably believes that disclosure of the information is necessary to prevent substantial injury to his client. He has "reported up" all the way to the Board of Directors. Therefore, under Rule 1.13(c) he could disclose the information to the State Department except for the fact that he had been asked to investigate these claims. Rule 1.13(d) provides that under such circumstances the lawyer may not reveal the client's confidential information even if all the other conditions of Rule 1.13(c) are met. **Answer (A) is incorrect** because there is no general authority to reveal client confidential information when a client has violated the law. **Answer (B) is incorrect** because Sam had been appointed to investigate the matter. **Answer (C) is incorrect** because there is no requirement that lawyers reveal a client's confidential information that the client has violated the law. Answer (D) is correct.

164. **The correct answer is (A).** The problem is that Ginormous is represented by counsel, and

normally there are strict rules about direct contact between an attorney and the employees of a corporate adversary. See Comment 7 to Rule 4.2. Those rules apply even if the represented "party" initiates the contact, so **Answer (D) is wrong.** See Comment 3 to Rule 4.2. The purpose of the prohibition on contact is to protect the represented party from overreaching. However, since Dash is an attorney, he is presumed to be capable of protecting himself and Ginormous from any attempt to overreach by Cindy. No consent of outside counsel is necessary, so **Answer (C) is wrong**, and **Answer (B) is wrong** because the contact is permissible. See ABA Formal Op. 06-443.

165.   **The correct answer is Answer (B).** Under Rule 7.5(a), a lawyer may practice using a trade name as long as it is not false or misleading and as long as it does not imply a connection with a government agency or with a public or private charitable legal services organization. Herman's name is none of these and is therefore permissible. **Answer (A) is incorrect** because trade names are permitted by Rule 7.5(a). **Answer (C) is incorrect** because the Model Rules do not purport to regulate taste in lawyer marketing. See Comment 3 to Rule 7.2. **Answer (D) is incorrect** because Rule 7.5(a) does explicitly address the circumstances under which lawyers are permitted to use trade names. Answer (B) is correct.

166.   **The correct answer is Answer (B).** Julie needs help, and a conversation with her former law professor would be an efficient way to obtain it. **Answers (C) and (D), however, are incorrect** because disclosure to an outsider is neither explicitly nor impliedly authorized by Rule 1.6. The purpose of Rule 1.6, protection of the client's confidential information, can be accomplished by using a hypothetical question that guards the identity of the client and the matter. See Comment 4 to Rule 1.6. An abstract, hypothetical legal question is not confidential. Only if the discussion would reasonably lead the professor to knowledge of confidential information would the discussion violate Rule 1.6. **Answer (A) is incorrect** because the hypothetical will keep the client's information confidential. Answer (B) is correct.

167.   **The correct answer is Answer (A).** Don is a former client of Allan. Allan may not undertake a new representation that is adverse to Don's interests if the two matters are the same or substantially related. To determine whether matters are substantially related, consider what information the lawyer ordinarily would have learned in the first representation and ask whether that information would be specifically useful in the second. Here, Allan ordinarily would have learned everything about Don's assets. The new proceeding is directly concerned with the existence and location of Don's assets. Allan has a conflict under Rule 1.9(a). If Allan has a conflict, Mitchell has a conflict under Rule 1.10(a). Don could waive the conflict, so Answer (A) is correct. **Answer (B) is not correct** because screening is not a solution to this type of conflict under the Model Rules. Compare Rules 1.10(a)(2), 1.11(b)(1), 1.12(c)(1), and 1.18(d)(2). **Answer (C) is incorrect** because the matters are substantially related. See Comment 3 to Rule 1.9. **Answer (D) is incorrect** because the only consent that will solve the problem under Rule 1.9(a) is the consent of the former client. Answer (A) is correct.

168.   **The correct answer is Answer (C).** Under Rule 1.12, a lawyer like Saul who has participated personally and substantially in a matter as a law clerk to a judge may not represent anyone in that matter, without the informed consent of all parties. However, under Rule 1.12(c), the disqualified lawyer may be screened so that the lawyer's firm can undertake that representation. **Answer (A) is incorrect** because the firm may not substitute as counsel without consent of all parties or a screen. **Answer (B) is incorrect** because there is another

way — the screen — for the firm to substitute as counsel without the need for informed consent of all parties. **Answer (D) is incorrect** because there are at least two ways for the substitution to be permissible. Answer (C) is correct.

169. **The correct answer is Answer (D).** Kerry has been burned by disqualifications as a result of conversations with prospective clients. Now that he knows of the risk, as long as he obtains informed consent of the prospective client, he can make an agreement with a prospective client before the interview that nothing he learns during the interview will prevent him from representing an adverse party and that he can use information from the interview against the prospective client. Comment 5 to Rule 1.18. Answer (D), therefore, is correct. **Answer (B) is incorrect** because he may represent an adverse party later even if he obtains harmful information, such as when the lawyer learns harmful information from a prospective client who has given informed consent to the lawyer doing so. **Answer (C) is incorrect** because of the word "only." Comment 2 to Rule 1.18 excludes people who blurt out their confidential information from the protections of the Rule, but that is not the only way to avoid disqualification later. **Answer (A) is incorrect** because just taking precautions will not necessarily protect the lawyer from disqualification, although it may protect the law firm from an imputed disqualification. Only Answer (D) is correct.

170. **The correct answer is Answer (D).** Under Rule 1.8(e), lawyers are permitted to provide only certain types of financial assistance to clients in connection with pending or contemplated litigation, and living expenses are not included. **Answers (A), (B), and (C) are all incorrect** because the Rule prohibits subsidies, loans, and guarantees for living expenses. See Comment 10 to Rule 1.8. Answer (D) is correct.

171. **The correct answer is Answer (B).** Contingent fees for criminal defense are not permitted. Rule 1.5(d)(2). The purpose of this prohibition is to avoid a divergence between the lawyer's interests in obtaining an acquittal and thereby earning a fee and the client's interest perhaps in pleading guilty. **Answer (C) is, therefore, incorrect.** Because Cindy also cannot acquire any literary or media rights to her client's story until her representation is complete, **Answer (A) is incorrect.** Rule 1.8(d). Although it is permissible for one person to pay another person's legal fees, the payment must be with informed consent of the client. Rule 1.8(f)(1). The agent paying the fee anonymously, as in **Answer (D), is, therefore, not an option.** Answer (B) is correct because it accurately states two of the limits on the fee arrangement that Cindy can make with this client.

172. **The correct answer is Answer (A).** Jack is holding property that both his client and the opposing party claim to be theirs. Under Rule 1.15(e), Jack's obligation is to hold the property separate until the dispute is resolved. **Answers (B) and (C) are incorrect** because there is a dispute about ownership. If either party clearly was entitled to the money, then under Rule 1.15(d) Jack would have to pay the funds to that party. While the funds are in dispute, however, Jack can pay neither party. **Answer (D) is incorrect** because the attorney cannot presume to be the arbiter of who is entitled to the money. See Comment 4 to Rule 1.15. Answer (A) is correct.

173. **The correct answer is Answer (C).** Delia suspects that her criminal defendant client is going to present false evidence, but she does not know that he is going to do so. Under Rule 3.3(a)(3), the lawyer could refuse to offer the evidence but for the fact that this is testimony by a criminal defendant. Under Rule 1.2(a), the decision to testify belongs to the criminal

defendant, and because Delia does not know that the evidence will be false, she will not be violating her duty not to knowingly present false evidence to a tribunal. **Answer (A) is incorrect** because the decision to testify belongs to Spike. **Answer (B) is wrong** because "narrative" testimony is one means for accommodating the right to testify with the lawyer's obligation not to knowingly present false evidence. Delia does not know this evidence is false, and therefore there is no need for the narrative. Delia can help her client just like she would any other client. **Answer (D) is wrong** because Delia will not be violating any rule of conduct to assist a criminal defendant client to testify when she does not know the evidence is false but merely suspects it. There is no basis for mandatory withdrawal. Delia must allow her client to testify. Answer (C) is correct.

174. **The correct answer is Answer (D).** Beau now knows that the plaintiff engaged in fraud related to a proceeding in which Beau was representing a client. Under Rule 3.3(b), Beau would have had the obligation to take reasonable remedial measures, including if necessary disclosure to the tribunal, if Beau had learned the information before the proceeding was concluded. Under Rule 3.3(d), however, his obligation ended when the proceeding concluded. It concluded when the time for appeal passed. See Comment 13 to Rule 3.3. **Answer (A) is incorrect** because the duty to act ended when the proceeding ended. **Answer (B) is incorrect** because Beau would have been obligated to take reasonable remedial measures while the case was pending if he knew that any party intended to engage, was engaging, or had engaged in criminal or fraudulent conduct related to the proceeding. The key is not that the conduct is in the past but rather that the proceeding has concluded. **Answer (C) is incorrect** because Beau's duty under Rule 3.3(b) to take reasonable remedial measure before the proceeding had concluded would have trumped his duty of confidentiality. Rule 3.3(c). Answer (D) is the correct answer.

175. **The correct answer is Answer (C).** Emery is in a difficult position because he is caught between his need to protect what he believes to be his client's constitutional right and his duty to obey the rules of the tribunal under Rule 3.4(c). He may need to disobey the rule to protect his client, but he cannot attempt to deceive the court and opposing counsel by remaining silent. An open refusal to comply with the rule on the basis that it is invalid is not be treated as attorney misconduct, and Rule 3.4(c) will permit Emery to take this course of action. Because Emery has this option, **Answer (A) is incorrect.** Emery does not have a conflict of interest, as stated in Answer (D), because Rule 3.4(c) gives him a way to protect his client and himself. **Answer (B) is wrong** because there is no special rule for disobedience of court rules when a constitutional right is involved. Answer (C) is correct.

176. **The correct answer is Answer (A).** Rule 3.1 imposes upon lawyers a limited "gate-keeping" role in litigation. Lawyers are not allowed to file cases that are frivolous, but a case is not frivolous just because the lawyer needs the discovery process to develop vital evidence. Nor is it frivolous to file a case that is not warranted by existing law but is supported by a good faith argument for the extension, modification, or reversal of existing law. **Answer (B) is incorrect** because Rule 3.1 does address the gate-keeping role, albeit in a different way than Federal Rule of Civil Procedure 11 and the state versions of Rule 11. **Answer (C) is incorrect** because the lawyer can file the case and then use discovery to gather the vital evidence. See Comment 2 to Rule 3.1. **Answer (D) is incorrect** because it is not frivolous to make good faith arguments to change existing law. Answer (A) is correct.

177. **The correct answer is Answer (C).** Under Rule 3.4(f), lawyers generally may not request

that someone refrain from giving information to another party unless the person is a relative, employee, or other agent of a client and the lawyer reasonably believes that the person's interest will not be adversely affected by refraining from voluntarily giving information. Here, the witness is clearly an agent of the client, so as long as this second condition is met the request is proper. **Answer (A) is incorrect** because it is enough for the witness to be an agent of the client. The witness need not be an employee. **Answer (B) is incorrect** because this request is explicitly permitted by the rules, even if it does impede the other lawyer to the extent that the other lawyer must employ formal discovery to obtain the evidence. **Answer (D) is incorrect** because it must also be true that the agent's interests will not be adversely affected by refraining from giving information voluntarily. Answer (C) is correct.

178. **The correct answer is Answer (B). Answer (A) is wrong** because no provision in the Model Rules of Professional Conduct directly forbids making threats to help a client in a negotiation. However, in some states it would be extortion to threaten to reveal the alleged fraud unless the client's husband agrees to a favorable settlement. In a state where it is extortion, Conrad would be engaging in misconduct under Rule 8.4(b) by committing "a criminal act that reflects adversely on the lawyer's honesty, trustworthiness or fitness as a lawyer." That would be misconduct even if all of Conrad's statements are "true" (but extortionate), so **Answer (C) is incorrect.** If it is not a crime, then the lawyer may make the threat, but this is not one of the decisions allocated exclusively to the client under Rule 1.2. To threaten to reveal the fraud would be a tactic to achieve the objective of the representation, a favorable settlement in the divorce. Under Rule 1.2(a), the lawyer must consult with the client about the means to be employed in obtaining a favorable settlement, but decisions on tactics do not belong solely to the client. **Answer (D), therefore, is not correct.**

179. **The correct answer is Answer (B).** As the mediator, Maria is acting as a third-party neutral. She represents no one in the mediation, but it is possible that unsophisticated, unrepresented parties like the tenant in this question may be confused about the mediator's role. Here, the tenant is asking this lawyer, in a private caucus, about the client's legal rights. Maria must make sure that this party understands her role and how that role differs from the role of a lawyer. Rule 2.4(b). Because just telling the tenant to seek advice of counsel would not accomplish this, **Answer (D) is wrong.** If Maria merely answers the question, or if she answers it but is sure to give the same legal assessment to the other side, the tenant may be confused and may believe that Maria is advising him as his lawyer. **Answers (A) and (C) are, therefore, incorrect.** Maria must explain her role to remove that confusion. Answer (B) is correct.

180. **The correct answer is Answer (D).** The sheriff is about to make a statement will definitely be disseminated in the media. Because it concerns damning evidence against the defendant, the statement has a substantial likelihood of materially prejudicing the trial. See Rule 3.6(a) and Comment 5(3) to Rule 3.6. This is, therefore, a statement that Oren could not make. **Answer (C), therefore, is incorrect.** His responsibility with respect to statements of law enforcement personnel is to exercise reasonable care to prevent statements that the prosecutor himself could not make. Rule 3.8(f). **Answer (A) is incorrect** because Oren has the obligation to use reasonable care to stop the sheriff from making this statement at a press conference. **Answer (B) is incorrect** because Oren's liability is not arising vicariously.

The sheriff is not making the statement at the direction of prosecutor, so Oren is not breaking Rule 3.6 "through the acts of another." Answer (D) is correct.

181. **The correct answer is Answer (B).** Under Rule 8.1(b), an applicant for admission to the bar must not fail to disclose a fact necessary to correct a misapprehension known to have arisen in connection with his application. Trevor had the duty to correct the record once he read the staff report. **Answer (A) is incorrect** because the Model Rules of Professional Conduct do not purport to establish standards for admission to the bar. **Answer (C) is incorrect** because it is not enough to have been truthful. Once he knew there was a misunderstanding, he had a duty to speak. **Answer (D) is incorrect** because the bar may discipline a lawyer for violations of Rule 8.1 that occurred before the lawyer was admitted. See Comment 1 to Rule 8.1. Answer (B) is correct.

182. **The correct answer is Answer (D).** Title insurance is an example of a "law-related service" under Model Rule of Professional Conduct 5.7. See Comment 9 to Rule 5.7. **Answers (C) and (A) are incorrect** because nothing in the Rules of Professional Conduct bars a lawyer from providing law-related services, even out of his law office. When the provision of such services is not distinguishable from the provision of legal services (as here), the lawyer is subject to the Rules of Professional Conduct even in connection with the law-related services. Rule 5.7(a)(1). **Answer (B) is, therefore, incorrect.** Answer (D) is correct.

183. **The correct answer is Answer (D).** Lawyers may enter into reciprocal referral arrangements with other lawyers if the arrangement is not exclusive and the client is informed of the existence and nature of the agreement. Rule 7.2(b)(4). Answer (D) is correct because an exclusive arrangement would not be permissible. **Answer (A) is incorrect** because informed consent of the client is not enough, although such consent presumably would satisfy the requirement that the client is informed of the existence and nature of the agreement. The arrangement could still be impermissible, however, if it is exclusive, and therefore it is not enough to say the client consented. **Answer (B) is incorrect** because reciprocal fee arrangements can violate Rule 7.2(b)(4) regardless of fee sharing. The purpose of Rule 7.4(b)(4) is to make sure referrals are being made with the best interests of the clients in mind rather than to maximize reciprocal referrals. **Answer (C) is incorrect** because under the conditions set forth in Rule 7.2(b)(4) reciprocal referral arrangements are permissible. Answer (D) is correct.

184. **The correct answer is (A).** Under Rule 7.5(b), law firms with offices in more than one jurisdiction are permitted to use the same name in both, but they are required to indicate the jurisdictional limits on the rights to practice of those attorneys not licensed in the jurisdiction where the office is located. **Answer (D) is wrong** because it is necessary to include statements such as "licensed only in [insert other state]" to avoid misleading clients about the lawyer's ability to practice in another state. **Answer (B) is wrong** because the firm can use the same name in both states. Rule 7.5(b). **Answer (C) is incorrect** because it is proper to list all the attorneys as long as the disclaimers appear. Answer (A) is correct.

185. **The correct answer is (C).** Ronald is planning to solicit a prospective client. That is usually not permitted under Rule 7.3(a), but the general rule does not apply when, as here, the lawyer does not have as a substantial motivation pecuniary gain. However, even otherwise permissible solicitations are impermissible when the prospective client has made known to the lawyer that person's desire not to be solicited. Rule 7.3(b)(1). That is exactly the case

here. **Answer (A) is incorrect** because it is incomplete. The original solicitation was permitted for this reason, but now even otherwise permissible solicitations cannot be made because the prospective client has made it known to the lawyer that the prospective client does not want to be solicited. **Answer (B) is incorrect** because the solicitation is impermissible if the prospective client has warned the lawyer off. It would also be enough if the solicitation involved coercion, duress, or harassment, but these are not necessary for the solicitation to be impermissible. **Answer (D) is incorrect** because it is far too general. Although generally lawyers may not solicit clients, doing so is permitted under certain circumstances, such as when the lawyer is not seeking pecuniary gain and when the person being solicited is a lawyer, a close friend or family member, or a former client. Rule 7.3(a). Answer (C) is correct.

186.   **The correct answer is (B).** Rodney must be careful about making any false or misleading communications about himself or his services. Even truthful statements about results achieved for others might mislead a reasonable person into believing that the lawyer can achieve the same results for them. See Comment 3 to Rule 7.1. **Answer (A) is incorrect** because truthful statements about fees are permissible. Comment 2 to Rule 7.2. **Answer (C) is incorrect** because the Model Rules of Professional Conduct do not regulate taste or dignity. Comment 3 to Rule 7.2. **Answer (D) is incorrect** because Rodney is allowed to state what types of work he does and does not do, as long as he is not stating or implying that he is certified as a specialist in those fields without a sufficient basis for doing so. Rule 7.4(a). Answer (B) is correct.

187.   **The correct answer is (D).** The attorney must be careful not to violate Rule 4.2, which forbids direct contact between an attorney and a represented party. One exception to this prohibition is if the contact is "authorized by law," which a contact made as part of an undercover investigation frequently will be. See Comment 5 to Rule 4.2. **Answer (B) is incorrect** because it is misconduct for an attorney to violate the Rules of Professional Conduct through the acts of another. Rule 8.4(a). **Answer (C) is wrong** because there are exceptions to the general rule against direct contact. One of those exceptions is the "authorized by law" exception. Rule 4.2. **Answer (A) is incorrect** because it is not enough to comply with the Constitution. The lawyer must also comply with the Rules of Professional Conduct. See Comment 5 to Rule 4.2 (last sentence). Answer (D) is correct.

188.   **The correct answer is (C).** Pauline is in a difficult position because she is dealing with an unrepresented person. She cannot give legal advice, but if she has to refuse to respond to questions from Liam then it is going to make the negotiations difficult. Comment 2 to Rule 4.3 makes it clear that lawyers like Pauline may explain their own view of the meaning of documents they have prepared, as long as they have explained that they represent an adverse party and do not represent the unrepresented person. **Answer (A) is incorrect** because a lawyer may not under Rule 4.3 give legal advice to an unrepresented person. **Answer (B) is incorrect** because Comment 2 allows a limited response as long as appropriate warnings are given. **Answer (D) is incorrect** because it would violate the Rules of Professional Conduct. Pauline herself could not be on both sides of this negotiation because she would have a conflict of interest under Rule 1.7(a)(1). If she has a conflict, then every lawyer in her firm has a conflict under Rule 1.10. Answer (C) is correct.

189.   **The correct answer is (D).** The other lawyer violated Rule 3.4(d) when he failed to make a reasonably diligent effort to comply with a legally proper discovery request by an opposing

party. Judith was the lawyer's supervisor, and she learned of the misconduct before the incomplete response was served, at a time when the consequences of the misconduct could be avoided, but did not take reasonable remedial action. Judith is therefore vicariously responsible for the misconduct under Rule 5.1(c)(2). **Answer (A) is incorrect** because Judith needs only to have direct supervisory authority over the offending lawyer. She does not need to be a partner. **Answer (B) is incorrect** because Judith can be responsible without ordering the conduct, by either ratifying it or by failing to take remedial action at a time when the consequences of the misconduct could avoided or mitigated. **Answer (C) is incorrect** because it would place strict professional liability on a supervising lawyer for the misconduct of subordinate lawyers. Rule 5.1(c) sets forth the limited circumstances under which such vicarious liability exists. It is not automatic. Answer (D) is correct.

190. **The correct answer is (A).** Answer (B) is incorrect because a lawyer cannot practice in a firm in which a nonlawyer owns an interest. Rule 5.4(d)(1). **Answer (D) is incorrect** because a lawyer cannot form a partnership with a nonlawyer if any of the activities of the partnership consist of the practice of law. Rule 5.4(b). **Answer (C) is incorrect** because of the possibilities raised by the correct answer, Answer (A). Under Rule 5.7, a lawyer is permitted to offer clients law-related services, including accounting services, subject to regulation. See Comment 9 to Rule 5.7. Because that is the lawyer's only hope for a "one-stop shop," Answer (A) is correct.

191. **The correct answer is (C).** Harold has violated Rule 4.2, through the acts of another (the paralegal), by having the paralegal circumvent the opposing attorney and speak directly to the victim. Under Rule 8.4(a), it is misconduct to violate the Rules of Professional Conduct directly or through the acts of another. **Answer (A) is incorrect** because Harold is not allowed to use others to violate the rules. **Answer (B) is incorrect** even though the paralegal was honest and therefore did not commit misconduct (on Harold's behalf) under Rule 8.4(c); what she did is nevertheless misconduct under Rule 8.4(a) because she violated Rule 4.2. **Answer (D) is incorrect** because lawyers are permitted to contact adverse parties directly, without invoking the formal processes of discovery, as long as either the adverse party is not represented or the adverse party's counsel gives permission for the contact to occur. Answer (C) is correct.

192. **The correct answer is Answer (A).** Under Rule 3.7, judges may participate in certain activities on behalf of certain organizations, including not-for-profit civic organizations. Planning fund-raising and management of the organization's finances are specifically permitted for such organizations. Rule 3.7(A)(1). **Answer (B) is incorrect** because judges may not engage in all extrajudicial activities. Rule 3.1 lists some of the circumstances under which extrajudicial activities are not permitted. **Answers (C) and (D) are incorrect** because planning for fund-raising and management of finances for not-for-profit civic clubs are two activities that are specifically permitted under Rule 3.7(A)(1). Answer (A) is correct.

193. **The correct answer is (D).** Judges are not permitted to serve as arbitrators or mediators or to perform other judicial functions outside of their official duties unless such activities are expressly permitted by the law of their jurisdiction. Rule 3.9. **Answer (A) is incorrect** because express permission under the law is required. It is not enough that the law of the jurisdiction is silent on the question. **Answer (B) is incorrect** because the judge may not render dispute resolution services, for economic gain or not, unless the law of his jurisdiction expressly permits it. Comment 1 to Rule 3.9. **Answer (C) is incorrect** because acting as an

arbitrator or performing any other judicial function outside of the judge's official duties is permitted with express authorization by law. Answer (D) is correct.

194. **The correct answer is (B).** Rule 2.9 governs ex parte communications with the judge. Here, the judge is communicating with a disinterested expert about the law, and the usual rule is that she may obtain written advice from such an expert with advance written notice to the parties as long as she gives the parties an opportunity to respond to the advice. Rule 2.9(A)(2). However, because this is a very particular type of advice — how the judge must act in order to comply with the Code of Judicial Conduct — the judge may seek the professor's advice and these special provisions about notice and an opportunity to respond do not apply. Comment 7 to Rule 2.9. **Answers (A) and (C) are incorrect** because the procedures that usually must be used when the judge seeks the advice of a disinterested expert on the law do not apply to this type of inquiry. **Answer (D) is incorrect** because some kinds of ex parte communications are permitted, and this is one of them. Answer (B) is correct.

195. **The correct answer is (C).** Under Rule 2.10(a), a judge is prohibited from making a nonpublic statement that might substantially interfere with a fair trial or hearing. **Answer (A) is incorrect** because even nonpublic statements can run afoul of the rule. These statements might well substantially interfere with a fair trial because the judge has gone on record, before all the evidence is in, with an opinion as to the guilt and veracity of the defendant. The judge might be reluctant to revise those views as the evidence develops (even though that is exactly what a fair and impartial judge would do) for fear that later reporting of his change of opinion would make her look indecisive, or even foolish. **Answer (B) is incorrect** because the judge is not expressing the type of personal bias that is disqualifying, a bias that makes fair judgment impossible. Naturally judges will form opinions about cases and witnesses as cases proceed. The judge can be fair and still think the defendant is a guilty liar. Maybe she is. The problem is not that the judge has an impression but rather that the judge's comments make it substantially harder to revisit that early conclusion. Similarly, **Answer (D) is wrong** because it is the making of the statements that creates the risk of an impartial hearing, not the source of the information that led to them. If the judge forms these opinions as the evidence proceeds but does not share them, the judge will be free to change her mind as the evidence dictates. That freedom is compromised by sharing her preliminary thoughts, regardless of the fact that she formed them only on the basis of the evidence. Answer (C) is correct.

196. **The correct answer is (A).** Rule 2.13 governs administrative appointments by judges, including appointments as assigned counsel. Under the Model Code, judges are not allowed to appoint major campaign contributors (the size of the disqualifying contribution is left blank by the Model Code for states to fill in as they deem appropriate), but there are exceptions. One of the exceptions is in Rule 2.13(B)(2), which allows a judge to appoint a contributor who is selected in rotation from a list of qualified and available lawyers. The lawyer is not receiving favorable treatment because of a campaign contribution but instead is simply the next lawyer in line. **Answer (B) is incorrect** because it misstates another of the exceptions. If the position was entirely uncompensated, then the contributions by the appointed lawyer would not matter. There is not an exception, however, for work that is compensated, even at below-market rates. **Answer (C) is incorrect** because there is an exception to the general rule for lawyers who come up in rotation. **Answer (D) is incorrect** because uncompensated work is not the only exception to the general rule against

appointing major contributors. Appointment in a regular rotation, as happened here, is another exception. Answer (A) is correct.

197. Sarah must either withdraw from the representation or do the work she feels she must do without expectation that the insurance company will pay her. Sarah owes Jane a duty to render competent representation. Rule 1.1. To follow the insurance company's orders would result in violation of that Rule, and therefore Sarah must withdraw from the representation under Rule 1.16(a) if the limits are to be observed. Sarah has the option to comply with her duty to render competent representation but must recognize that the insurance company may not compensate her for those efforts. See ABA Formal Op. 01-421.

198. All fee agreements, including modifications, must be assessed for reasonableness at the time they are made. No circumstances have changed except that the lawyer has begun to fear that he never should have taken the case on a contingent fee. Carter is therefore seeking to change the fee arrangement solely benefit himself at a time, the eve of trial, when the client may feel like there is no other choice but to agree to the new arrangement. This new agreement is almost certainly unreasonable, and it is therefore a violation of Rule 1.5(a) to make the agreement for, charge for, or collect the renegotiated fee. See ABA Formal Op. 11-458.

199. Rule 1.5 forbids lawyers from making agreements for, charging, or collecting an unreasonable amount for fees or expenses. Under that rule, the firm would not be permitted to charge more than the actual cost to the firm of the disbursements on the client's behalf unless the practice was disclosed to and agreed to by the client. The firm is attempting to create an undisclosed profit center, and as a corollary to its duty not to charge unreasonable fees or expenses, it may not collect more for a "disbursement" than was actually disbursed without client consent. ABA Formal Op. 93-379.

200. Dirk complied with his responsibility to "report up" the corporate misconduct that was putting his client, UDD, in jeopardy. He was fired for that, and in some states there is a public policy exception to the general employment at will doctrine that might enable Dirk to recover for wrongful discharge. Under Rule 1.6(b)(5), Dirk is permitted to reveal confidential information of his client to establish a claim between him and his client, UDD, to the extent that Dirk reasonably believes it is necessary to do so.

201. What Lillian has learned is obviously confidential under Rule 1.6(a). Lillian is bound to keep it to herself unless she has authority to reveal it or an exception under Rule 1.6(b) applies. None of the exceptions apply, so the question is whether informed consent of the client is the only kind of authorization that will enable Lillian to reveal the confidential information to her staff. It is not. Rule 1.6(a) also provides for "implied authorization in order to carry out the representation," and revelations within the law firm are impliedly authorized unless the client instructs the lawyer to keep the information confidential even from her staff. See Comment 5 to Rule 1.6.

202. Wilhelmina must reveal the death at the status conference, if not before. Although presumably Wilhelmina would never make an affirmative misrepresentation that her client was alive (doing so would clearly violate Rules 4.1 and 3.3(a)(1)), her situation now is more complicated. Under Comment 1 to Rule 4.1, "[m]isrepresentations can also occur by . . . omissions that are the equivalent of affirmative false statements." To continue to deal with

opposing counsel as if her client was not dead is the equivalent of a continuing misrepresentation that he is alive. Similarly, not to reveal this event to the court would in effect be a continuing misstatement of fact in violation of Rule 3.3(a)(1). Wilhelmina must reveal her client's death. See ABA Formal Op. 95-397.

203. Lawrence may contact the first two but not the third. Rule 4.2 forbids Lawrence from contacting someone who is known to be represented by counsel in the matter without the consent of the other lawyer. None of these people have an individual lawyer, so the only problem would be if any of them are off-limits because the corporate defendant is represented by counsel. Comment 7 to Rule 4.2 answers the questions. A former constituent of a represented corporation is fair game. The other two are still employed by the defendant, but the lawyer may contact anyone who does not regularly consult with the organization's lawyer concerning the matter, does not have authority to bind the company in the matter, and is not someone whose act or omission could be imputed to the organization for purposes of civil or criminal liability. The low-level employee who had nothing to do with the accident is not in any of these categories and could be contacted. The driver, of course, is someone whose acts or omissions could be imputed to the corporation for purposes of civil liability, and therefore he may not be contacted.

204. The lawyer is obligated to abide by a client's decisions concerning the objectives of a representation and to consult with the client about means. Rule 1.2(a). This is an instruction about means. It is also an instruction that the attorney need not follow. Comment 1 to Rule 1.3 states that the "lawyer's duty to act with reasonable diligence does not require the use of offensive tactics or preclude the treating of all persons involved in the legal process with courtesy and respect." It is within Leon's professional discretion to choose not to conduct the litigation in an unpleasant manner.

205. Clint may only seek to avoid an appointment for good cause, under Rule 6.2. One circumstance that is identified by the rule as "good cause" is when the representation is likely to result in a violation of the Rules of Professional Conduct. That is the case for Clint. He would likely be violating Rule 1.9(a) if he represented Justin. "Big Man" is a former client, and Justin's interests are likely to be materially adverse to "Big Man's" interests in this case. Justin is a low-level dealer who can likely make a deal if he agrees to give information about the "higher-ups." Furthermore, the cases are substantially related because they are both about the same drug conspiracy, and Clint would ordinarily have learned from "Big Man" information that would help Clint help Justin in this case. Because Clint has a conflict under Rule 1.9(a), there is good cause for him to seek to avoid the appointment under Rule 6.2(a).

206. Albert may ghost-write the pleadings without telling the court. Albert is prohibited from making false statements of fact to a tribunal, but in ghost-writing the pleadings Albert is not making any statements to the court. He has made no representations of any kind about the source of the pleadings, and therefore he is not being dishonest under Rule 8.4(c) (misconduct to be involved in deceit or misrepresentation). Nor is he violating Rule 3.3(a)(1) (false statements of material fact to a tribunal). Albert is free to render anonymous assistance. ABA Formal Op. 07-446.

207. Rule 5.4(b) forbids a lawyer from forming a partnership with a nonlawyer if any of the activities of the partnership consist of the practice of law. This is the rule that prevents

multidisciplinary practice, and it is intended to ensure that the traditional professional duties of lawyers, such as loyalty and confidentiality, are not compromised by the participation in a law firm of a partner who does not understand or appreciate the need for these duties. Here, however, both partners are lawyers, and so presumably that concern disappears. There is nothing to prevent the brothers from forming their partnership and operating as they plan to do. They need to be cognizant of Rule 5.7, which regulates the provision on law-related services like the title insurance, but they may form the partnership.

208. Rule 5.5 governs multijurisdictional practice of law. Daren wants to engage in a temporary activity related to pending litigation. Rule 5.5(b)(2) would permit Darren to take the depositions if Darren were taking them for a case in his home state or for a case for which he was admitted to appear by court order (pro hac vice) or reasonably expected to be so admitted. Here, however, Darren is to have no further involvement in the case. His activities are still authorized by Rule 5.5(b)(2), however, if the lawyer he is assisting — the boss — has been admitted in the third state to appear in the case pro hac vice or reasonably expects to be so admitted.

INDEX

INDEX